Billion Dollar Muslim

Why We Need Spiritually Inspired Entrepreneurs

To Abdullah and Bilal.

May you become the movers and shakers of this world, with great success in this life and the hereafter. Amen!

KHURAM MALIK

K HURAM MALIK

Irada Abdul-Hadi

Cover design by
Saad M. Ansari of Pluto Republic

DEDICATION

With special thanks to Donald Trump without whom this book wouldn't have been written so soon. And to Batman, who must be a Billion Dollar Muslim.

CONTENTS

LIVING BY THE PHYSICAL AND SPIRITUAL LAWS

THE MOST OVERLOOKED DAWAH OPPORTUNITY OF OUR TIME:

SUNNAH AS A BEST BUSINESS PRACTICE

THE AGE OF WISDOM:

POWER PLAYS FROM PAST TO FUTURE

FOREWORD

Since childhood, we Muslims have been conditioned to focus on our studies so we could get a "good" job, a respectable job, a job that Muslim parents can be proud of and boast about to their friends. We have been told to focus on a career that will be attractive to our future spouse or a job that will be accepted by a certain clique of friends.

Traditional jobs may be perfect for some, but for the Muslim entrepreneur -- who has a certain drive and passion, who comes from something other than the standard mold, who is never satisfied with the status quo and is always yearning for something bigger in life -- the traditional job becomes a shackle.

The traditional job limits your potential. Its restrictions prevent you from becoming the something bigger and greater that you yearn to be. The traditional job restricts your life in so many ways from location, position, and even pay. Once you have hit the "ceiling" in your job, attained the highest position you can achieve, and earned the highest pay the company is willing to pay you, where else is there to go?

What guarantees do you even have from your employer that you will even get a raise, or that you will receive your next bonus or even if your job will still exist next month?

Think about that.

And now, think about this:

On the flip side of that traditional job coin, there is another option, and if you break out of these molded expectations and take the risks that are innately natural to you, if you give yourself the permission to remove those shackles and take the chance to build your own destiny and put your trust in your Creator, amazing things can happen.

As children we were conditioned to have limiting beliefs. We were asked, "Honey, what do you want to be when you grow up?". But the real question is "What changes do you want to make in the world and in people's lives?". This is the kind of question that will broaden our horizons and open our minds to the limitless possibilities that can fulfill our hearts, minds and our futures.

Faisal Farooqui, CEO and Founder of FaisalFarooqui.com

ACKNOWLEDGMENTS

With thanks to Ramiz Ali, Zanib Mian, Faisal Amjad, Hodan Ibrahim, Imran Shah, Imran Iqbal, Asim Lone, Irada Abdul-Hadi and Kelli Law.

To my mother for her many duas and for instilling ambition in me by teaching me that I'm on this earth to change the world.

To my father for showing me what it means to be a man of integrity and honour.

And a special thanks to my wife who was the one to suggest I write this book in the first place after struggling to find material on entrepreneurship in Islamic bookstores.

The greatest thanks of course, belongs to His Majesty Allah Subhana wa ta'ala, without whom none of this was imaginable let alone possible. Nothing happens without His leave.

This book is written as a series of mini-essays that you can dip in and out of at any point. Unlike a typical book, each essay is written independently in its own right.

1 CHAPTER

WHY I WROTE THIS BOOK:
PLANTING THE SEEDS OF MUSLIM
ENTREPRENEURSHIP

"From the signs of the completeness of a person's intelligence is his having highness of aspiration. And I have not seen in the numerous poor qualities that a person can have, anything as poor as a lack of desire to succeed in those who are able to achieve perfection."

Ibn Al-Jawzi

My name is Khuram Malik. To clients and colleagues, I am known as The Strategist — a person that helps organisations with strategies for growth. I've been in entrepreneurship since I was 16 years old. I wrote this book to share my experiences of how taking a spiritual approach to entrepreneurship helped me with my goals. This book is not intended as an exercise of fiqh or the do's and don'ts of Islam in business, but rather as a spiritual guide on what has worked for many and what can work for you.

I want to change the way Muslims think about business. I want to export the best tenets of the valley mindset (explained in the chapter Leading the Way), excellence in morality and the pursuit of higher truths to Muslims around the globe. I want Muslim businesses to be leaders in creating organisations with more humanity while pushing the envelope of human achievement.

My greatest worldly wish is that Muslims create well-loved and well-respected brands that become the next household name. I want Muslim entrepreneurs to be true market leaders and innovators, to use their success and wealth for positive social change.

As one brother said to me once I told him I'd made intention to write this book:

"You've been in this game a long time. Sure you've had your ups and downs, but that's all part of the game. You have unique experiences and alhamdulillah, Allah has blessed you with knowledge. You really understand entrepreneurship, and you understand how to apply sunnah to it. Plus, you're up to date with the new, emerging world order. You're the only person that I can trust to give me the right perspective on my business ideas and how I should go about implementing them. You need to share that knowledge with the world. Allah has given you a gift. Share it".

*****

When I was 14 years old, my dad decided he wanted to invest the small amount of money he had saved from his 9 to 5 on the stock market, but he wasn't sure where to start. Being a geek (at a time when it wasn't yet fashionable to be one), my dad told me to read the brochures for the stockbrokers and figure out how to open an account and get started. I spent a few days during my summer holidays reading the brochures and sharing what I had learned with my mum. My mum then fed back the information to my dad at work. The day came that we were ready to get started with our first stock trade. My dad signed the paperwork, filled in the application form, and off we went and made our first trade.

Two years later, working in tandem with my mum and dad, we turned £2000 of his investment into a portfolio of just under £20,000 with a few up and downs in between. I'll be honest, it was mostly guess work, and I gladly admit I got lucky, not least because I was emailing financial consultants (when 95% of the UK population didn't even know what the word email meant), sharing investing ideas with them and getting investment tips and ideas. They thought they were speaking to a middle-aged, seasoned investor at the other end (i.e. my dad). Little did they know they were emailing back and forth with a 14-year-old whose voice hadn't even broken yet.

I was fascinated by computers and technology in general from a very early age. When I was 16, while all my school friends were getting jobs at McDonald's and other famous stores on the high street, my dad helped me get a job in a small independent computer shop, where the owner of the shop agreed to teach me how to build a PC and install Windows in exchange for a minimal wage. After building 500 PCs over the course of a year with my bare hands, my friend Andrew and I decided we'd try selling PCs ourselves from home.

So Andrew and I spent a week cleaning out my mum and dad's garage, painting it white and setting up a show display with my own personal computer. My father wasn't very happy about me using my own computer as the display since he'd spent more than two months of his salary to pay for it to help me with my education.

Andrew and I spent a few nights distributing leaflets in the local residential areas, and a week later a young man came to the house looking to buy a PC. He left Andrew and I with a deposit of £200 asking us to build the PC and have it delivered to his house on Sunday night. By Sunday night, Andrew and I made a net profit of £286 on our first PC. For a skinny, shy and spotty teenager, that was millions.

That night, as I was walking to my bedroom, I overheard my father say to my mum "I think I should help those kids sell those PCs. They need an adult to look after them"

My dad would go to work each day and tell his colleagues, "My son can build computers". Bill Gates' vision of a "Computer on every desk" had yet to be realised, and everyone was interested in buying a new computer at this time. The internet was still just a buzzword, and parents were looking for a computer for their son or daughter to help them with their school or university education.

I spent many weeknights and weekends delivering PCs to the houses of my dad's colleagues and other friends of his in our local community. We started running out of space to build PCs at home and demand was still increasing. Everyone at every dinner party and wedding was talking about computers. Dad wanted to capitalize on this and decided to open a computer shop with one of his associate's brothers. The idea was that this business partner would manage the shop day to day, while my dad put up the initial funds to start the business. My dad decided that it was better if I weren't too heavily involved so I could focus on my university degree.

Unfortunately, his new business partner never turned up the first day of business, and there was no option left but for me to be called in. I would attend my university lectures in the morning, and then in the afternoon walk half an hour down to the computer shop and serve customers, build PCs, order new stock from the suppliers, do some basic bookkeeping and take deposits to the bank, six days a week. It was a lot for an 18-year-old to learn and manage, but thankfully I had some guiding inspiration.

My paternal uncle had a friend whose own computer business had collapsed by this point, but at the peak of his career he had been doing about £30,000 a day in revenue.

This was the man that had built my first computer. I saw him often around the time he built my PC and also while starting the new shop, so I learned a lot of the ropes from him. That experience combined with my curiosity allowed me the momentum to start picking things up, bit by bit. The fact that I loved computers and loved exploring new ideas helped propel me a great deal. Also in my favor was my confident habit of always asking lots of questions.

If I found a trade magazine and found a new supplier, I would just call them and say, "Right, what do I need to do?" And they'd say, "You need to fill out the application form or you need to do this or you need to do that" and then I would just try it. Many times I would get it wrong. Often, new suppliers would realize they were speaking to an inexperienced "kid" and push me off the phone. In those instances, I would tell my dad the supplier wasn't playing ball, to which my dad would respond by calling them from work and making sure the account got opened. After that, they'd be back to doing business with me!

Although our first computer shop only broke even, a few of my father's peers decided to get in on this trade as well. My dad would have me pop round to their shops every now and again to share what I had learned: how to do the bookkeeping, how to open accounts with suppliers, how to deal with customers and so on. A skinny, spotty, slightly less shy teenager was teaching middle-aged men how to run their computer businesses!

Once I came back from my internship in Cambridge (more on that later), we started with our second shop. By this time, we had learned many lessons about many areas of the computer retail industry. We'd gotten better at hiring good staff; we'd gotten better at persuading customers to choose us over big brand names; we had learned how to negotiate better with suppliers, and we'd learned how to get more customers through the door.

That year, our computer shop did just under £1 million in revenue (approximately $1.5 million). I was just 20 at the time.

***

For a long time, it was really hard for me to explain why I got into entrepreneurship. I could explain the how, but never the why.

I guess if I had to boil it down to one thing, it was this: I saw a man that would look forward to going to work every day, feeling happy at work, and making more money than my mum and dad combined at half their age. He worked hard and played hard.

On the other hand, I saw my parents: I saw my dad constantly worrying about paying the mortgage and bearing the burden of the grief his boss would cause him at work. My dad constantly suffered from institutional racism, and on many occasions my mum was brought to tears at work, despite being a very sincere, enthusiastic and hardworking teacher. My mum gave great care and attention to her students. I could never fathom why anyone would ever put themselves through this kind of emotional torture just to pay the bills. To me it never made any sense.

Besides, I loved computers.

When I finished University, a leading telecoms company in the UK was undergoing a major global merger in Europe. The same telecoms company went on to win many important telecoms deals in the Middle East after the success of their European merger. That was the first time I truly started to understand the kind of influence big business had around the world. I also learned the value of infrastructure and got some idea of how these businesses impacted economies, society and politics. Though I had a lot more to learn, I definitely started to recognize the possibilities. I decided this was my life purpose: to create these infrastructures and to create platforms from which society would benefit. But I didn't know where to begin. Yet somehow I knew that if I stuck to entrepreneurship, I would eventually find my way there.

That remains my key driver today: using entrepreneurship as the launching pad to benefit society. It's a highly over-used cliché, but it's not just about the money after all. Millionaires create financial freedom for themselves, so they can afford the nice car and the nice house. Millionaires change their own world; billionaires change the world.

2 CHAPTER

THE GREAT LONGING FOR CHANGE:
IT'S TIME TO GET OUT OF THE 'RAT RACE'

"Normal is getting dressed in clothes that you buy for work, driving through traffic in a car that you're still paying for, in order to get to a job that you need so you can pay for the clothes, car, and the house that you leave empty all day in order to afford to live in it".

Ellen Goodman, American Journalist

I often ask new brothers and sisters I meet the following question:

"If you had all the money you could ever possibly need and knew you would never have to work for money ever again — what would you do with your life?"

And, of course, the first answer is always "I would quit my job". Few are happy with their day job and see it purely as a means to an end. The second thing people often say — after mentioning they'd buy a house and a nice car, and maybe do a little something for their parents — is that they would do something for the deen, or the greater good. Unfortunately, no matter how highly paid our jobs are, few of us ever attain the real wealth to actually pursue our dreams.

***

Zulekha spent over three years, midway through her office administration career, to study to become a teacher. After she got her degree in teaching, she secured a job as a school teacher. Due to her sheer hard work, she was promoted a few years later. Now, she starts work at 7.30 a.m., teaches kids until lunchtime, catches up with administrative work during lunch, and then goes back to teaching the kids until the end of the school day. After that, she does the necessary paperwork until around 6.30 p.m. and gets home around 7 p.m. She feeds her husband and kids, takes a quick break and then finishes off the necessary school work at night. She finally heads to bed around 11 p.m. The next morning, she starts the same cycle all over again. Most weekends she has to dedicate at least half a day to catching up on paperwork, and sometimes, she feels obliged to work all weekend in order to accomplish what needs to be done.

She once told me that when she goes to sleep at night, she often can't sleep because she's worrying about all the things she has to get done for work the next day. When she wakes up in the morning, the thoughts occupying her mind are exactly the same as when she went to bed the night before. She said she often feels like she didn't sleep because her mind is always racing.

And, despite her own hard work and that of her husband, there are many times throughout the year when they worry if they'll be able to make ends meet.

This kind of story might be an extreme example, but it's not a total anomaly, and these kind of stories are common throughout the world. Our brothers and sisters are working hard in jobs with little satisfaction and a paltry reward. When we're so spent in our careers and occupied with taking care of our families, it leaves little mental and emotional capacity to contribute towards the greater good.

Wealth isn't measured purely by our bank balance; it is also the freedom to do with our lives what we want. Thankfully the Millennial generation is starting to recognise this.

3 CHAPTER

TILL DEBT DO US PART:
THE NEED FOR FINANCIAL RE-EDUCATION

"I am a member of a species that thinks working five days a week for 40 years to pay off a debt on a bank's computer screen is freedom".

Unknown

Yusuf, a highly intelligent pupil came over to the UK with his father from Iraq in the early 90's when he was just seven years old. His father came to earn his PhD and brought his family with him as he was planning on a stay of seven years. Yusuf was a clever pupil but as he progressed through high school, many teachers told him they didn't think he would go far in life. That affected him at a very deep and personal level.

When Yusuf was 14, his father completed his PhD. With his father's student visa now expired, Yusuf and his family had no choice but to go back to the Middle East.

Twenty-five years later Yusuf applied for a PhD in linguistics in the UK. By now, he was married with children of his own and worked his way, in his war torn country, to secure a place in the UK. He was over the moon when he got confirmation that he'd be going back to the UK. He had great memories of his time there as a child, with his friends and with life in general in the UK. By his own admission, he had rather nostalgic memories of living in the UK and projected romantic notions of how life was going to be going forward; but, in reality, he was desperate to get out of an ever more unstable Iraq. He felt his PhD was going to be just the ticket he needed.

After four years in the UK, Yusuf got his PhD and was now over £60 thousand in debt. His student visa was coming up to expiry, but the situation in Iraq was even worse than when he had left. His parents had already been forced to flee their home due to the arrival of rebels, and Yusuf was facing a similar fate. He pleaded with his sponsors to help let him stay, but he had only two options. He could either return to Iraq and be placed in a job chosen by his sponsoring institution, or he could pay off the £60 thousand debt. With two kids and a third on the way and no source of extra income in the four years he'd been working on his PhD, Yusuf had no choice but to go back to Iraq.

By the time Yusuf arrived back in Iraq, his academic paper had been published, and Yusuf had achieved great academic acclaim. He was well known in the linguistics academic community and had reached the heights of academic success.

Several months after Yusuf's paper was published, Yusuf called his friend in the UK who was an advisor to CEO's in the construction industry. Yusuf asked for his advice on running a construction business. A little perplexed, since Yusuf was a linguistics specialist, his friend asked him why he was suddenly changing career paths, especially after the long and arduous road he'd taken with his career up till now.

Yusuf replied: "For the last 15 years, I've done nothing but grind and grind in study and where has that gotten me? I've got three kids, and I'm still worrying about being able to put food on the table. I've worked so hard, aced all my exams and presented my dissertations; I've poured my heart and soul into getting my PhD, but look at me! I'm broke, and I'm desperate to get out of this country."

Despite Yusuf's incredibly impressive credentials, there was nothing that he could do for himself.

His total disillusionment was clear when he continued: "I don't even feel like a man anymore, and this is the dream that we're selling to our kids: 'Get a PhD, get high scores, make your mark and then the world will be at your feet.' That is absolutely not true! It's not true for anybody!"

***

As a global population, we're heavily dependent on academic systems. There's a certification program for everything. If there's something we don't know or want to learn, we assume that getting certification in that area will give us the success we're looking for. A mindset understandably driven by what we see of staple subjects such as medicine and accountancy. But such guaranteed success isn't the case in other areas.

Understanding our personal and intimate relationship with money is incredibly important in generating wealth. It's the crucial topic that is missing on most MBA curriculums. It's discrepancies such as this that cripple ambitious people's chances of success.

We have a huge generation of university students that struggle to manage their own finances when they leave university. Poor financial habits follow them for the rest of their lives because the correct financial education was never given.

Most MBAs do not go on to create successful businesses. By the time they complete their MBA, the world has often moved on and they've not had enough practice in the 'real world' to hone their skills, and by that time they're already deeper in debt.

There are no standard courses that teach us how to have a loving relationship with our spouse or how to perfect our relationship with our Creator or how to define and maintain balance in our relationship with money. Yes, these courses exist in niche areas, but they're not mainstream subjects nor do they appear on standard education curriculums. Yet, they're the very topics that can help us lead fulfilling lives. Instead, standard curriculums busy us with memorising the periodic table; rote knowledge which, quite frankly, doesn't add to our sense of fulfilment

Discussing money and financial slavery (amongst others) has been a taboo topic in our communities for too long. We have an ever-growing population of youth that suffers from chronic depression, burgeoning financial debt, health issues and a distinct lack of purpose. A huge crisis is brewing right under our noses; our community is drowning in debt. We're creating financial martyrs to our own detriment as a community and as a society. It's this very habit that creates the deadlock that we spend the rest of our lives trying to get out of.

Most of our inclination towards this debt-based and deadlock mindset started through the introduction of industrialism into our deprived and torn countries. Industry was seen as the first beacon of hope and our first taste of possible liberation. Instead it manufactured a mindset of dependency on capitalists who only sought to benefit from our labour, and we bought into a false dream of jumping on the academic and "good job" bandwagon to career success.

This is why entrepreneurship is no longer a choice but a necessity. Our modern education systems are no longer adequately preparing our youth for the future. The rapid pace of technology, globalization and ever-developing economic models means that unless we take charge of this space and become leaders in this area, we are going to be left in the dust. As a group, we will be inadequately prepared and entirely ill-equipped for the future. Some of the waves of change that are about to come are going to be so gigantic, that if we don't appropriately prepare ourselves, we're going to be tossed against the rocks so hard we'll never recover. This preparation can only come from embracing entrepreneurship en masse.

It's time to break out of the industrial mindset and favour entrepreneurship over employment, or at the very least, choose important start-ups over corporates, because once somebody goes into debt their thinking faculty is seized and reverts from thinking how to grow to focusing just on how to survive. And with such a mental handicap, we will never prosper.

A "good job" was, and is still, seen as the ultimate and best path to personal fulfilment, yet there is no such thing as a good job. In fact, things are worse now than ever before. If we're going to lose sleep every night worrying about debt, and whether we'll have a job to go into the morning, why not channel that energy into self-determination and into our own businesses? After all, we need to start somewhere.

With entrepreneurship we can stand up and reclaim our power. Regretfully, most of us fail to recognize that power even exists in the first place.

It reminds me of the stories from the slave trade, best explained by Malcom X's speech at Michigan University on January 23,1963:

"So you have two types of Negro. The old type and the new type. Most of you know the old type. When you read about him in history during slavery he was called "Uncle Tom." He was the house Negro. And during slavery you had two Negroes. You had the house Negro and the field Negro.

The house Negro usually lived close to his master. He dressed like his master. He wore his master's second-hand clothes. He ate food that his master left on the table. And he lived in his master's house-- probably in the basement or the attic--but he still lived in the master's house.

So whenever that house Negro identified himself, he always identified himself in the same sense that his master identified himself. When his master said, "We have good food," the house Negro would say, "Yes, we have plenty of good food." "We" have plenty of good food. When the master said that "we have a fine home here," the house Negro said, "Yes, we have a fine home here." When the master would be sick, the house Negro identified himself so much with his master he'd say, "What's the matter boss, we sick?" His master's pain was his pain. And it hurt him more for his master to be sick than for him to be sick himself. When the house started burning down, that type of Negro would fight harder to put the master's house out than the master himself would.

But then you had another Negro out in the field. The house Negro was in the minority. The masses--the field Negroes were the masses. They were in the majority. When the master got sick, they prayed that he'd die. [Laughter] If his house caught on fire, they'd pray for a wind to come along and fan the breeze.

If someone came to the house Negro and said, "Let's go, let's separate," naturally that Uncle Tom would say, "Go where? What could I do without boss? Where would I live? How would I dress? Who would look out for me?" That's the house Negro. But if you went to the field Negro and said, "Let's go, let's separate," he wouldn't even ask you where or how. He'd say, "Yes, let's go." And that one ended right there.

19

So now you have a twentieth-century-type of house Negro. A twentieth-century Uncle Tom. He's just as much an Uncle Tom today as Uncle Tom was 100 and 200 years ago. Only he's a modern Uncle Tom. That Uncle Tom wore a handkerchief around his head. This Uncle Tom wears a top hat. He's sharp. He dresses just like you do. He speaks the same phraseology, the same language. He tries to speak it better than you do. He speaks with the same accents, same diction. And when you say, "your army," he says, "our army." He hasn't got anybody to defend him, but anytime you say "we" he says "we." "Our president," "our government," "our Senate," "our congressmen," "our this and our that." And he hasn't even got a seat in that "our" even at the end of the line. So this is the twentieth-century Negro. Whenever you say "you," the personal pronoun in the singular or in the plural, he uses it right along with you. When you say you're in trouble, he says, "Yes, we're in trouble."

But there's another kind of Black man on the scene. If you say you're in trouble, he says, "Yes, you're in trouble." [Laughter] He doesn't identify himself with your plight whatsoever."

Malcom X's speech strikes a chilling parallel to the financial slavery we find ourselves in today.

When I first thought about moving on from the business my dad and I built together, I went to an uncle for advice. I still remember his exact words from where I was sitting in the back of his brand new Mercedes "get a job for a year or two and first get some experience".

A year later, having done a corporate job for about nine months, I got similar advice from another successful entrepreneur: "I think you should get an MBA, then get a high profile job, and then think about going into business".

Just replace "house slave" with the modern "financial slave" in Malcom X's speech, and suddenly the alarm bells start ringing louder and louder.

.

4 CHAPTER

LEADING THE WAY:
FOCUSING ON HUMANITY

"Never doubt that a small group of thoughtful, committed citizens can change the world. Indeed, it's the only thing that ever has."

Margaret Mead

An online shoe retailer that one man started from his bedroom has a 365-day returns policy. A woman can buy a pair of shoes in January and, if she so chooses, can return them ten months later — "no questions asked". The best bit: free shipping both ways.

The customer service is exemplary. Employees are told not to rush any calls and to spend as long as they need to "deliver happiness". One customer service call lasted nine hours.

In another case, a lady ordered six pairs of shoes for her ailing mum who was in hospital, hoping one of the pairs would cheer her up. Two weeks later, her mum's health deteriorated further. Distraught, the lady decided to return all six pairs. When customer service found out the reason for return, they sent her mum a bouquet of flowers wishing her a speedy recovery and agreed to pick up all six pairs directly from the hospital without any shipping cost. They also upgraded the lady to a VIP account. It's no wonder their customers are always ecstatic.

The employment policy is unusual too. New hires, regardless of their job title or position, have to spend a minimum of one week doing customer service. That includes new managers, programmers and even accountants. No one goes scot-free. After their training period, new employees are presented with an option. Salary for time spent so far plus a $2000 bonus if they decide to accept the option and leave. This offer stands throughout the entire training and a few weeks beyond. New hires have a unique opportunity to make an educated choice about their own happiness and decide whether they can fully commit to the company.

This retailer, known as Zappos, has over 1500 employees and was acquired by Amazon in 2009 for $1.2 billion.

"For me, my role is about unleashing what people already have inside them that is maybe suppressed in most work environments. I view my role more as trying to set up an environment where the personalities, creativity and individuality of all the different employees come out and can shine" (Tony Hsieh, CEO of Zappos).

***

A teenager that wanted to be a graphics designer struggled to get paid design work. No one would take him seriously since he was just a "kid". He approached a number of small businesses in his local area, but the first thing people would ask him was what he'd managed to do for others. It was a chicken and egg situation. One day he decided to offer his design talent to a non-profit for free. He figured it would be a good way to do something for the greater good while also building up his portfolio to establish credibility. The owner of the non-profit loved his work and decided to recommend him to others. One thing led to another and bit by bit, paid work started coming in.

Starting to wonder if there was some mileage in a 50/50 business model since non-profit work led to referrals, the teenager decided to incorporate this idea into his business model. After the very first non-profit work, the teenager decided that he would dedicate 50% of his time to non-profits and the rest to businesses. People saw the quality of his work and talent, and suddenly he wasn't just a "kid", but a guy that could create great logos and leaflets.

The teen graphic designer thoroughly enjoyed the work he was doing. He got better at his craft over time and decided to enter a design competition for the MTV awards. He came first in the MTV design competition and word spread even faster about his talent. More and more work started pouring in.

His design agency has now grown to over 350 contractors and volunteers worldwide, with clients such as UNICEF and Disney. The agency, "VeryNice", still operates on a 50/50 business model.

By 2014, VeryNice had invoiced just under $2 million in pro bono work.

***

A leading food processor with over 400 employees that processes over 25% of California's tomato production has no managers. There are no job titles, no promotions and no directives from 'above'. Instead the company practices the art of self-management, and every employee makes decisions largely based on their commitment to others. Every employee has access to company money and can spend it as they see fit. If a junior employee needs to write a cheque for $2000 for new stock or items that will benefit the business, he or she can feel free to do so. Best of all: no one has a boss.

That's not to say there isn't an overall leader or lack of a vision. Far from it. But simply to say it's not a typical 'command and control' hierarchy. There's no one to report to and no 'typical' performance appraisals and reviews. Instead of being told what to do, employees are self-directed and look at what needs to be done.

This food processor, Morning Star Company, has annual revenues of over $700 million.

***

Just like Zappos' concern for customer satisfaction, VeryNice's charitable outreach and Morning Star Company's vision of employee equality, there are many other examples of companies with innate practices that seem agreeable to Islamic teachings. The most curious thing, however, is that none of them were founded by a Muslim. Any average Muslim observer would be forgiven for thinking they were though.

This unconventional approach with a strict commitment to making customers happy, making employees happy and creating meaningful change in the world is often touted as the "valley" mindset (from Silicon Valley) . The Silicon Valley Framework, or the "valley" mindset, is not in fact limited to the geographical area of Southern California, where the name was first coined.

It can be observed in other parts of the world such as Canada, Australia and New Zealand, to name just a few countries with well-known hubs for enterprise and innovation. The framework uses first principles to say: We've always done things "this way" or things have always been done in "this and that" way but now let's re-think those practices. It gives rise to companies that fundamentally question the way society has been functioning or solving an existing problem up to now.

This approach is intent on creating enterprises with a greater sense of humanity, something Muslims were well known for in Islam's golden age. I've always admired this valley mindset because of its striking parallels to Islam. Going against the accepted norms is exactly what our father of Islam, Ibrahim (peace be upon him) did when he challenged the way society ran in his time by blindly following what their "fathers and forefathers" had always done.

When the late Peter Drucker, a highly respected and revered management scholar, said that the fundamental purpose of a business is to solve societal problems, many in enterprise realised this could only be done by asking the right questions about how society currently functions.

But confronting societal problems directly is not the valley mindset's only striking parallel to Islam.

24

This mindset often demands that companies choose the best people to solve these problems and be the best at solving them. The best companies of the valley aggressively commit to pushing the "envelope" while making things better for everyone: employees, customers, the environment and society at large. This is in striking contrast to corporate behemoths often found to be driven by greed.

When a new start-up founder that subscribes to the valley mindset asks herself how she's going to go about solving the problem for her customers, she's simultaneously telling herself:
"My employees have to be happy as well, our customers have to be happy. Everything has to be as good as it can be." Striving to do one's best in every aspect is a very Islamic thing.

Islam encourages a high level of excellence and integrity in all areas of our lives: the Messenger of Allah (peace be upon him) has said, "Verily Allah has prescribed ihsan (perfection) in all things... " (Muslim). As Muslims, we are encouraged to do our very best in whatever we do, whether it be raising a family, cleaning the house, writing a book, or establishing a business. We must realize that the impact of our words and actions can be far-reaching, thus when we give our very best effort, we hope, in sha Allah, to see the best results.

It follows then that the Muslim entrepreneur is obligated to give his best effort and in the best of manners in every pursuit. Without question, this applies to perfecting business practices in every aspect from treating employees well, having a generous attitude towards customers and striving to improve society.
Islam demands we seek the higher truth, to aim high, pursue excellence and to choose the best suited people to offer solutions to society. The Prophet Muhammad (peace be upon him) surrounded himself with men and women of the highest integrity and the greatest allegiance to his purpose. When specific skill sets were needed he (peace be upon him) would assign people to tasks according to their strengths and expertise. For example, during the building of the Prophet's Mosque in Medina, the Prophet (peace be upon him) recognized that Talq ibn Ali Al-Yamami, may Allah be pleased with him, was skilled at mixing and applying the plaster; so, the Prophet stopped him from carrying the bricks and ordered that Talq be in charge of the mixing and application of the plaster.

Thus, business, and by extension the choice of entrepreneurship, is a perfect vehicle for the mu'min to make the world a better place.

5 CHAPTER

HEY HO TO THE STATUS QUO:
IF YOU WANT TO CHANGE THE
WORLD, YOU HAVE TO CHANGE THE
STATUS QUO

*"The mind of a slave asks, 'Is it legal?' " The mind of the freeman
asks, 'Is it right?' "*

Anonymous

Ibrahim had been hired as a contract cleaner for a law firm. When
he first started with them, they gave him some background on the
business. They explained they had a very high success rate in the
courtroom, and some of the senior lawyers had decades of experience.
Over the next few months, as he performed his cleaning duties during
the day, he saw this in action. Many of the senior lawyers would take
on cases that seemed impossible and sometimes unethical (to defend)
but yet they'd return from the courtroom having won.

27

A couple of months into the contract, Ibrahim noticed that some of the supplies he needed for the next month had not arrived. He was worried he wouldn't be able to complete his cleaning duties. Thus, he advised the finance department to set-up recurring billing so that supplies would arrive on time each month. A couple of months later, as he noticed the window cleaning equipment wasn't as good as he expected it to be, he advised management to change suppliers.

One day as he invoiced the firm for the previous month of work, he noticed payment had been withheld. It turned out the CEO had instructed the finance department to withhold payment. The CEO felt that Ibrahim had caused the law firm a "major loss" by advising them to order supplies for cleaning equipment for the entire year. In reality brother Ibrahim never advised them to pay for the entire year, but only to set the payment to be automatic for each month.

In the grand scheme of things, the loss to the firm was very minor, and Ibrahim was not at fault. The CEO wanted someone to blame for this loss, and therefore started a dispute with him and inappropriately withheld payment.

Humans are a product of their habits and environment. Our actions and the environment we choose directly affect our heart. There is a clear connection between a person's occupation and the qualities of their character.

In the case above, the management team at the law firm had gotten so used to winning any dispute without ever questioning the ethics of it; an intellectual blind spot — that they hadn't stopped to think about the ethics of their actions. Their hearts were severely affected and so was their rationale.

It's important to develop our habits carefully and be selective about our environment. We can choose habits and environments in our everyday lives that can support our iman and our heart. Yet being so discerning usually demands that we reject accepting things just as they are or just as they have always been done. Entrepreneurs, by their very nature, often choose a life of rejecting the status quo in every facet of their lives.

I often meet entrepreneurs, that not only reject the status quo (or seek to change it) in the area of business they choose to be in, but often seek to change their personal lives too. I've met many entrepreneurs that have very different personal attitudes, habits and lifestyles compared to the 'Joe public' from very early on in their lives. The kind of food they choose to eat, the way they choose to approach their work and productivity, their attitude towards health, travel and exercise. You name it; they're non-conformist in every way.

It's this kind of non-conformist attitude that drives them to create change.

Right now, Bill Gates is using a huge part of his financial might to wipe out malaria in Africa. There has been no single foundation that has tackled this problem with this kind of dedication. He's also invested heavily in education and is on a mission to change the way the world approaches children's education. In fact, he is so committed to this that he invested heavily in Khan Academy, a site that provides online education to children around the globe with over 5,000 free instructional videos and has more than 10 million users per month.

But even Bill Gates started with goals that were less philanthropic, such as the goal to have a PC on every desk.

We don't know much about Steve Jobs' philanthropic efforts, but what we do know is he couldn't stand the current status of computing at every major juncture in his life and always sought to change it. Apple was the first to create many new markets. It was the first company to make personal computing a reality, and the first to offer smartphones and tablets with real practical merit. This kind of drive and achievement is only possible when you reject the status quo.

As one part-time imam — with his feet firmly planted in reality — said to me:

You have to partly get the psyche of surrounders and their pulse, without letting it be your pulse. Because you can transcend it. Truth be told, most adults struggle at that. Partly because we're schooled into it. The only people that can do it effectively though that I've seen are Entrepreneurs, who live by rules, while knowing how not to see them as black and whites that their life and enterprises are bound by. The other is the true believer, on the path of Ibrahim (peace be upon him). Because if they are of the few Muslims who try and replicate or follow the path, they realise they aspire to have core belonging solely to Allah, they don't need anything, or dare I say, anyone else. Powerful and transformative. You're not mentally bound by anything, let alone a bell ringing at class time. But you follow the convention because it's fine and works, but you see past it."

6 CHAPTER

THE PRESSING CASE FOR ENTREPRENEURSHIP: AN OPPORTUNITY FOR A GOLDEN ERA

"He who finds a new path is a pathfinder, even if the trail has to be found again by others; and he who walks far ahead of his contemporaries is a leader, even though centuries pass before he is recognized as such."

Attributed to Ibn Khaldun

As I write this paragraph, I count seven separate requests from different people encouraging me to donate to a worthy cause. The number of social causes, both national and international, demanding the Ummah's attention seem to increase in number every day. It seems as the financial demands increase so do the need for human resources.

Whenever I do the first strategy session with a client, I always ask them what their immediate challenge is and what the long term objective is. When I first started offering marketing advice to non-profits, I found myself constantly addressing the same challenge with each non-profit founder I spoke to. Things got to the point where, I stopped asking non-profits what the challenge was and, often jokingly, started each session with the line "Don't tell me; you need to raise funds, yes?"

The second challenge they always cite is "lack of resources".

Granted, part of this problem has much to do with the non-profits' ability to market themselves and to tell their story. These challenges may paint a large part of the picture, but are by no means the complete story.

Real social change takes a huge amount of resources, and if our ummah is spent in their careers, we will never be able to make the kind of changes we dream of. The intrinsic potential of entrepreneurship to deliver these resources is one of the very reasons we should have more Muslims pursuing entrepreneurial ventures.

The time has come for every Muslim family to aspire to have at least one wealthy entrepreneur in the household.

Sadly, in my last 15 years in business, I've observed very little humanity amongst Muslim businesses. The valley mindset is unheard of, and at best, is a pipe dream. The commitment to happy customers and happy employees is nothing but mere lip service. The profit incentive seems to override all else, and ironically, little do they realise that adopting a framework of humanity and building businesses on the virtues and admirable qualities exemplified in the sunnah of Prophet Muhammad (peace be upon him) is the very thing that will generate profit far more than the current way of doing business.

In our first marketing strategy session regarding her jewelry business, Samena said something like the following to me:

"I hope you won't judge me for saying this, but I have purposely chosen not to market my products to Muslims, even though, there's big demand in our community for this kind of jewelry. It's just that I feel our own community is the worst when it comes to business. They're the first to complain about price, and the first to haggle. These are upmarket items, and I want to market them to the high-end. I just don't think our community has either the appetite or the appreciation for what I am creating. I'd just rather save myself the heartache. I know it's a horrible thing to say, and I do feel guilty for saying it, but I've put a lot of love into creating these products, and I don't want to devalue the brand. You know I even had a non-Muslim create my website because the last brother that tried to make the website for me caused me nothing but heartache. It was really difficult working with him, and it always seems to be difficult to work with anyone from the Muslim community when it comes to business. So I just went to a nice English lady, and she's been a joy to work with. I'm very happy with my website and glad I found her."

Suffice it to say, I didn't judge her for her perception of the Muslim community. She wasn't the only person to carry these sentiments, and she certainly won't be the last.

Another brother, with extensive experience in the charities sector, who works with many other non-profits and businesses alike told me this "secret".

"Our own community is the worst when it comes to management. At my last company (a major charity), even in this modern era of mobile apps and what not, we were still taking donations to the charity by writing credit card details on paper.

We don't keep our promises, we don't turn up on time, we constantly blame each other, and we completely lack any kind of discipline or professionalism. If the public knew how much money is lost to poor management in these organisations, they would probably stop donating.

And don't get me started on what we're like as employers! One Muslim media outlet I know of has a key for the kitchen and toilet. The employees have to ask permission for the key when they want to use either of these facilities. And that's not the worst of it. If an employee comes to work late, the employers will count all the minutes accruing for late attendance at the end of the month, and deduct it from that person's salary. It's the most draconian way of doing business, and I can't stand it."

Looking at problems Muslim communities around the world have faced in the last 30 years, and then comparing those to the last 20 years, then to the last 10 and then to our current situation, what we find is that not only do we continue to suffer, but the problems have gotten progressively worse.

Charities still turn to wealthy entrepreneurs for the majority of their donation fund while on the whole discouraging entrepreneurship. A very strange paradox indeed! Our institutions and organisations run incredibly inefficiently, and we constantly fail to meet our long term objectives. This situation has not improved at all.

Yet, as a community, if we had embraced entrepreneurship en masse even as recently as 20 or 30 years ago, we would have been able to make the changes we need by now. By now we would have had enough practice at the entrepreneurial game, at running organisations, at knowing what it takes to bring a large group of people together and create a change in society.

***

On August 28, 1928, in the Scottish Highlands, began the secret story of oil. Three men had an appointment at Achnacarry Castle - a Dutchman, an American and an Englishman.

The Dutchman was Henry Deterding, a man nicknamed the Napoleon of Oil, having exploited a find in Sumatra. He joined forces with a rich ship owner and painted Shell salesman and together the two men founded Royal Dutch Shell. The American was Walter C. Teagle and he represents the Standard Oil Company, founded by John D. Rockefeller at the age of 31 - the future Exxon. Oil wells, transport, refining and distribution of oil - everything is controlled by Standard oil.

The Englishman, Sir John Cadman, was the director of the Anglo-Persian Oil Company, soon to become BP. On the initiative of a young Winston Churchill, the British government had taken a stake in BP and the Royal Navy switched its fuel from coal to oil. With fuel-hungry ships, planes and tanks, oil became "the blood of every battle".

The new automobile industry was developing fast, and the Ford T was selling by the million. The world was thirsty for oil, and companies were waging a merciless contest but the competition was making the market unstable.

That August night, the three men decided to stop fighting and to start sharing out the world's oil. Their vision was that production zones, transport costs, sales prices - everything would be agreed and shared. And so began a great cartel, whose purpose was to dominate the world, by controlling its oil. Four others soon joined them, and they came to be known as the Seven Sisters - the biggest oil companies in the world.

In The Secret of the Seven Sisters, a well-researched documentary produced by Al-Jazeera, the series highlights how the oil barons made secret agreements and colluded to starve the world of its natural resources to satiate their own greed. What's staggering however, is that, despite their prowess, the oil barons' plans didn't go well every time, but they did have enough time to practice.

As a group of Muslims, if we today decide to take the "fight" to the oil barons to oppose their tyranny, we would find ourselves at a huge disadvantage, purely due to their sheer volume of practice over us. Nothing else. They can outdo us with their experiential edge over us because we have limited ourselves to only understanding how to do our "jobs," and we haven't made any effort to understand how to influence and change society.

But we have to start somewhere, and at some point. The longer we keep telling ourselves we can never compete, the worse the situation will get. The sooner we start; the sooner we can gain the experience we need to compete.

***

Entrepreneurship creates wealth; the freedom to pursue the more meaningful activities that you want in life. Rather than working a lifetime looking forward to retirement, dreaming of the things you want to do in life, and being controlled by the things you have to do (paying bills, fulfilling others' agendas etc.), you can establish the means, through entrepreneurship, to start living the actual life you want sooner.

During an interview at Stanford University, Oprah Winfrey was asked about her phenomenal success; Oprah said: "The key is to know yourself. To be aware."

Our ability to achieve our purpose is fundamentally dependent on understanding ourselves. It is essential that we nurture wholesome and complete relationships with ourselves, with others and, most importantly, with our Creator. The integrity of these three relationships determines our ability to truly realize our purpose. Absurdly, these very three criteria are never taught in school. Instead, through revised histories and grossly excessive academia, school teaches us our relationships with authority, with common law and with survival. We are indoctrinated into a life of subsistence, rather than initiated into a life of the pursuit of excellence.

How can entrepreneurship develop an understanding of one's self and foster thriving and meaningful relationships on each of these levels?

Firstly, as an entrepreneur, one is forced to recognize one's own strengths and weaknesses. Truly successful entrepreneurs must identify and cultivate their own individual passions and expertise. They must challenge the very "demons" inside themselves, the vices or shortcomings that keep them from improving. The introspection required to discover one's own strengths and faults, and the discipline necessary to improve on the former and minimize the effects of the latter enables the individual to grow and foster a relationship with the self thus, leading one to realise his/her grand purpose.

Secondly, creating change in society is wholly dependent on our ability to nurture relationships with others, but if we're in a menial job sitting behind a desk, getting by with very little, barely interacting with others, then we'll never be able to impact society the way that we want. Modern life has already reached the point of hyper-individualization: we no longer talk to our neighbours; we barely talk to our parents; and we pass our daily commute with barely a smile to the person next to us on the train, forget about saying hello or asking them where they're headed. Life has become all about the individual pursuit. In stark contrast, entrepreneurship forces you to pursue not just what's best for yourself, but what is best for others such as customers, employees and suppliers. Entrepreneurship turns that discerning eye outward.

Lastly, uncertainty about the future or the outcome of a decision is a stepping stone in building a relationship with our Creator. This is true because overcoming uncertainty often necessitates a leap of faith or establishing a trust or reliance in something higher. Jobs create a certain psychological bubble of security. As individuals in these secure bubbles, we only have to be concerned with matters that extend as far as our job. We don't have to deal with or worry about the stress that goes beyond our remit; those concerns are left to our seniors, our employers, or others higher in rank. This falsely perceived "safety net" limits our concerns to our pay cheque at the end of the month. For the entrepreneur, this is not the case. Living outside the illusion of a safe bubble, the entrepreneur has to rely on herself for making sure she has a pay cheque at the end of the month. She has to take those leaps of faith that are necessary to deal with all matters that relate to her business. The courage and ability to take those leaps of faith comes through building the relationship with the Creator and relinquishing the unknown and uncertain into the trust of the One who does know and is certain. As an entrepreneur, you are forced to turn to something bigger than yourself to support and guide you along the way: that entity is Allah Subhana wa ta'ala.

***

In entrepreneurship there's no limit. If you want to create a small business that only serves ten people a month, then so be it. But, if you want to create a business with a product that envelops the globe, there may be people that will tell you it can't be done, but no one can actually stop you. In an ordinary job, your employer can put a stop to your dream very quickly via their authority over you.

A popular business consultant, who had worked with many billionaires over the last several years, was asked: "What is it that billionaires do, and what is it that they understand that the rest of us don't?"

His response was: 'Having worked with other billionaires, it basically comes down to this one simple quote from Steve Jobs, "Once you start to realize that this world and everything around you was created by people no smarter than you, you can change it. You can influence it. You can build your own things that other people can use" '.

What this quote means is that it's not about IQ, or about academic achievement. These people that have created the amazing things that have come before us have just been driven and consistent in their efforts to have an impact on the world. That same drive doesn't exist in a full time job. In a job we do just enough to get by, to get paid at the end of the month. We don't do enough to change the world. At least not in most jobs.

***

If we're going to take the ummah back to the golden era, this way of doing business has to change. As Muslims, we should be the first to lead the charge in making happy customers, happy employees and creating meaningful change in the world.

But, unless we start building the capacity for an entrepreneurial climate and making it easier for the next generation, nothing will change.

7 CHAPTER

THE GOOD SHEPHERD:
ENTREPRENEURSHIP CREATES WELL-ROUNDED PEOPLE

"A human being should be able to change a diaper, plan an invasion, butcher a hog, conn a ship, design a building, write a sonnet, balance accounts, build a wall, set a bone, comfort the dying, take orders, give orders, cooperate, act alone, solve equations, analyze a new problem, pitch manure, program a computer, fight efficiently, die gallantly. Specialization is for insects."

Robert A. Heinlein

In the Arabian Peninsula, around the time of the Prophethood, the wealthy would often pay shepherds to take their sheep out to graze in the wilderness for days at a time. If the shepherd didn't bring all the sheep back unharmed, he didn't generate repeat business. A good shepherd was reliable and dependable, as we know was the case with Prophet Muhammad (peace be upon him) and many prophets before

41

him.

Shepherds had to learn to be incredibly self-reliant and resourceful. They had only themselves to depend upon while out in the wilderness alone. Sheep are not easy to manage, and they can often wander astray making them vulnerable to wolves. Managing sheep teaches one finesse in leadership and management.

Spiritual directives from Allah Subhana wa ta'ala often have parallel practical applications. For instance, we pray salah to purify our soul, but in order to pray we must purify our physical body too. Wudhu is the practical counterpart to the spiritual directive of salah.

For the prophets, taking care of sheep was the practical counterpart to learning how to lead and manage large groups of people.

Abu Huraira (may Allah be pleased with him) narrated that the Prophet (peace be upon him) said, "Allah did not send any prophet but he shepherded sheep." His companions asked him, "Did you do the same?" The Prophet (peace be upon him) replied, "Yes, I used to shepherd the sheep of the people of Mecca for some Qirats [coins]" (Bukhari).

So, we learn from this hadith that every prophet Allah Subhana wa ta'ala sent down, earned his living as a shepherd. Every prophet was "groomed" before prophethood, as a shepherd.

These days, it's not so practical (no pun intended) to choose being a shepherd as a vocation. The only practical equivalent that I can think of in the modern day, other than perhaps a career in the armed forces, is entrepreneurship. Entrepreneurship is undoubtedly the next best thing.

One could get a job as a team leader, project manager, or consultant in a large organisation and feel they've found the practical equivalent, but the reality is that the degree to which these positions demand self-reliance and resourcefulness is nowhere near the same. This is true for the simple reason that neither team leader, project manager, nor consultant takes primary responsibility for the development and growth of the organisation as a whole. (Their responsibility for growth is often limited to a single department or project).

***

Wasim chose to go into freelance consulting because although he had been paid well in his corporate job, he always felt like something was missing. He'd been working long hours for the last several years and spending many days and nights away from his family. His daughter was growing fast, and he felt he was missing out on her childhood. His corporate job often required him to spend four nights in Glasgow at the company head office, away from his daughter in South England, and some months he'd have to travel into Europe for as many as 10 days at a time.

The money was good, but he just felt like a "cog in a machine". A very well-oiled one at that, but a piece in a machine nonetheless. He wanted to do something for himself, something where he didn't feel obligated to make useless small talk with colleagues or where everyone pretended to like each other. All the pretentiousness of the corporate world had finally taken its toll, and Wasim had decided to carve out his own path.

But Wasim struggled in his freelance work. Even though he had acquired a lot of experience in his corporate job, he had only contributed a piece of the puzzle. Wasim had never experienced the sales process from beginning to end. All sales had been spearheaded by Mark in the contracts team, and Dustin had dealt with all legal arrangements over in the New York office. Wasim, himself, only ever got involved with the project when the sale had been won and it was time to deliver. While having honed and strengthened a specific skill-set, Wasim found that he was still lacking some much-needed training and know-how.

That's the frustrating issue with being a specialist. If you can find a hole to fit into, you can be a very useful Lego piece and rewarded generously, but when you go it alone, you have to acquire the skills for the whole Lego set; you must become the Master Builder.

Even though entrepreneurship may seem scary, tiresome and difficult, especially in today's unrelenting financial climate, the truth is that entrepreneurship can be very liberating and fulfilling. And given the current increase in job uncertainty, I would argue that it is perhaps necessary.

8 CHAPTER

ENTREPRENEURSHIP IS THE GAME-CHANGER:
THE 'IZZAH WE SEEK AS UMMAH WILL COME FROM AN ECOSYSTEM OF ENTREPRENEURSHIP

"The people who built Silicon Valley were engineers. They learned business; they learned a lot of different things, but they had a real belief that humans, if they worked hard with other creative, smart people, could solve most of mankind's problems. I believe that very much."

Steve Jobs

In her article, Know Your Worth: If We Don't Know, We Can't Grow Our Community, Nicole Kenney points out that the dollar remains circulating within Jewish communities for an average of 20 days as opposed to Black communities where the dollar circulates only six hours. What this means is that because there are more established Jewish businesses and enterprises to bring in revenue, the Jewish community's economy is stronger, and their financial resources are greater. So entrepreneurship is the game-changer, and this is a lesson the Jewish community recognised much quicker than the rest.

I still remember how it took me by surprise when I learned that in many Jewish homes entrepreneurship is actively encouraged. One entrepreneur from New York said this in his video interview:

"At family gatherings, all the grown-ups were always talking about business. They were always sharing ideas with each other on how to grow their businesses, and I just couldn't wait to get out of school so I could start my own. As soon as I got out of college I held down one job for about six weeks then told myself I'd had enough. After that I learned how to make money selling clothes and started one business after the other after that. I've never looked back". — New York Entrepreneur

In Jewish homes entrepreneurship is more readily found. A co-founder of a successful start-up that hails from a Jewish family in Central Europe says:

"My dad and I always discussed business when I was growing up. He taught me many things, such as one should always give away their best ideas and that success is all about getting better and better at each thing you do every day. When I went to college, as I was studying, I also tried many business ideas from my dorm rooms, in my free time, in between lectures and on weekends. Instead of getting a part-time job like most students, I thought I'd try my business ideas to learn how to make money. Dad taught me that the most important skill I needed to learn first was to figure out what people wanted. I would often call my dad and we'd chat about how I was making progress in study and in business. I learned a lot in my college years, not just in the classroom but also in my dorm" - Silicon Valley Start-up Co-Founder.

It is somewhat interesting that in his book Entrepreneurship: Critical Perspectives on Business and Management, Norris F. Krueger states that "In the case of the Jews, 2000 years of refugee status and large numbers of credible examples make the entrepreneurial act almost an expect role" (Vol. 4, p. 106).

But it's not like this in Muslim homes, despite our own history of emigrating and being forced into "refugee status". We need to wake up and recognise and encourage the entrepreneurial spirit in our youth.

In my own home, the biggest emphasis was on study and academia. My parents never held back in facilitating education and always went out of their way to make sure I had access to everything I needed. Traditional education isn't enough anymore.

***

A family friend of ours, whose father had passed away when he was still studying, told me his father used to run a business, but never wanted him to go into business. He told me what his father said:

"I don't ever want to see you in business. I don't want to see you running a corner shop, or a market stall. I want you to stay well away. You study hard, and you get yourself a good job. I have worked hard in business so that you can get a good education"

It saddens me to learn most Muslim parents think this way. The world has changed, and we need to learn to adapt.

There are some silver linings here and there however, and while I have lost faith in modern education systems more than most, Zanib Mian brings a nice balance to the equation: "I really feel that having an entrepreneurial father gave me an entrepreneurial mindset, but my education equipped me with the skills to in sha Allah succeed in it."

But upbringings like Zanib's are still the exception rather than the rule.

Entrepreneurship needs much more encouragement in Muslim homes. Our youth should be encouraged to consider the path of the entrepreneur as a viable career choice.

***

A sincere Muslim that has wealth is more capable than one that doesn't. A sincere Muslim that is strong, in terms of self-reliance and ability in acquiring knowledge on his own, is more capable than one that isn't. Financial wealth is a great catalyst, but other driving factors help too. Those that affect meaningful change.

In fact, in a recent talk by Sheikh Tawfique Choudhury, he mentioned the case of the rise of entrepreneurship in South Africa, in which he explained that although the percentage of Muslims in South Africa is approximately 4% of the population, the number of businesses owned by South African Muslims is in fact much greater (approximately 37%). He says in his talk: "For many years, the state of the Muslims in the West was so-so. Every nation was just 'plodding along', but in the last decade or so, Muslims in one country have leap-frogged their counterparts in all other nations, and that country is South Africa. Since South African Muslims own a large number of businesses now, this gives them much better representation in the country as a whole." He then goes on to say to the parents. "Enough Doctors. We have plenty of doctors now, enough with the doctors. We need more entrepreneurs".

Practical change in society is driven by two main contributors: policy makers and doers.

Entrepreneurs are doers. Entrepreneurs often take primary responsibility for creating tangible change. Change you visibly see. Fundamentally, what I refer to is changing infrastructure and systems. Every type of practical change merits the development of infrastructure and systems in one form or another. Further developing a country needs improved telecommunications infrastructure, property development, transport links and so on. These situations demand all kinds of infrastructure.

If it weren't for Howard Hughes, transcontinental flights wouldn't have been what they are today. If it weren't for Bill Gates and Steve Jobs there would be no computers or smartphone. We'd still be working with mainframes or typewriters. And if not for Elon Musk, who knows how long it would have been before we kick started a nationwide charging network to make fully electric cars a reality.

These are entrepreneurs that have contributed greatly to human progress. Entrepreneurs are the 'movers and shakers' of the world.

Sure, the actual work is performed by labourers, but the reality is that these things don't happen unless there is a leader that forms the team, sets the vision, and executes the plan. That said, entrepreneurs are more than just managers. They're value creators; people that know how to create 'something out of nothing' and know how to work with a high degree of uncertainty. Labourers and managers alone - due to the limitations and restrictions of their roles - often can't overcome many of the challenges that are faced in situations of uncertainty and unknowns.

***

At a recent non-profit event, the key speaker and founder of the charity presented some of the great things the charity had been able to achieve in such a short period of time. Everyone in the audience applauded and was pleasantly surprised by what had been accomplished. The speaker then went on to explain his previous background and the audience learned that he was a former, proven entrepreneur. He went onto say that they'd been able to achieve so much, so quickly because they had brought the corporate mindset to the planning and execution of the charity.

Learning that the charity had achieved so much due to applying an entrepreneurial mindset was no surprise to me, but I do wonder if it surprised others. I've often found much resistance to the corporate mindset in the non-profit sector. On some level, I can understand; corporates are often associated with bureaucracy and niggardliness, but such a mindset has plenty of upsides too. The skills that the entrepreneur acquires throughout their lifetime are highly transferable.

Yet we don't practise entrepreneurship en masse despite the benefits and hikmah (wisdom) we can derive from it.

We're taught many things at school, but what we're never taught well enough is the art of self-study. Critical thinking skills are severely lacking in modern education. It is a far greater problem in the less developed nations, but developed countries are no strangers to it either.

In a detailed study of why some nations develop faster than others, one key point was that nations that actively encourage and facilitate entrepreneurship develop faster and prosper more than others by great magnitude. In addition to this, they found that a largely multi-disciplinary population was the essential prerequisite for this growth in prosperity. Well-rounded people facilitate change better than specialists.

Broadening our knowledge and skillsets is a value conventional wisdom hasn't taught us, but it is an advantage entrepreneurs have developed as a natural consequence of entrepreneurship.

We must learn to become multi-disciplinary individuals in order to create change. Change demands this, and entrepreneurship facilitates this.

I wish there were more true Muslim entrepreneurs because when you really understand entrepreneurship, you truly understand the hikmah of it. This hikmah is something that you can't just observe and garner from others, and furthermore, it's not something you can truly benefit from, at least in my personal opinion, until you commit yourself to practising entrepreneurship holistically.

9 CHAPTER

BREAKING MYTHS ABOUT ENTREPRENEURSHIP: IT'S THE WAY FORWARD NOT A BACKUP PLAN

"If you think being an entrepreneur is risky, try working for someone else for forty years and living off social security".

Steve Mehr

For many, Entrepreneurship is often seen as a last resort. It is often looked down upon as a case of: "If you can't find anything else to do, if you can't become a doctor, or a lawyer, then maybe at that point, you should consider entrepreneurship."

If we're really honest with ourselves the reason why we consider entrepreneurship a last resort has more to do with our parents that than our current generation. Many of our parents emigrated to the west and had great difficulty finding ordinary jobs due to their lack of education. They also compounded the effects of naturally occurring racial segregation within our communities when they resorted to starting their own businesses as a means of earning money. The impacting result was that they weren't just socially secluded because they weren't hanging out in bars and pubs, but even occupationally, they were separated from most of the general society.

They were running corner shops and small factories where they mostly employed or served their own. Subconsciously, this continued to reinforce the general inferiority complex – that feeling of being an "outsider". What better, at least for the parent with the need to feel accepted or included, than for their son or daughter to be an accepted, inclusive member of western society through a "respectable job" in the medical or legal fields.

So, for many of us, the real reason our parents wished for us to be "Doctors and Lawyers" was a chance for them to feel included by virtue of having their sons and daughters established in professions deemed "well respected" and accepted in society.

Even for those whose parents were not emigrants looking to find acceptance, there was the allure of high-paying professions which promised to set their children up for life. But this hope, too, was nothing short of false. False, because if we took an honest look at what these professions pay, we would quickly realize that there are far better ways to earn money. So our parents' pushes and nudges into medicine or law weren't about guiding us to career choices offering us personal satisfaction and enjoyment or even quickly gained financial freedom. Sadly, our parents' misplaced hopes for acceptance and financial security has burdened the lives of many from the new generation with a mountain of debt and unfulfilling, meaningless careers. If anything, the recession of 2008 proved very well that there's no such thing as long term job security.

True entrepreneurship was never given a chance, yet the conversation couldn't have been more relevant. But to understand why it was and still is an important discussion, we first have to dissect what entrepreneurship really is.

Unfortunately, these are the common assumptions and misconceptions of self-employment. Entrepreneurship is often defined as the art of giving oneself a difficult job to pay the bills, where the pay cheque is decided by one's accountant, rather than one's employer. The real definition of entrepreneurship couldn't be more different.

Natalie Sisson, also known as The Suitcase Entrepreneur, opens our eyes to the real potential of the true entrepreneur: "The entrepreneur is seen as the agent of change and the maker of movements".

Using one's skills and ability resourcefully to create meaningful change in society while also making wealth for oneself and others is real entrepreneurship.

The opportunity to pursue entrepreneurship today is greater than it has ever been. Anyone anywhere simply with a computer and an internet connection can build a profitable business. The beauty of entrepreneurship is that you can do what you love and what you excel at and simultaneously serve others by providing solutions to their common problems, in whatever niche or area that may be. And of course, you can make whatever income you desire and have a chance to live a life of freedom with your time and money. This is a global revolution. Be a part of it and take advantage of this limitless opportunity, in whatever capacity you are able and willing. (Farzan Parupia, MuslimExpert)

Entrepreneurship is an amazing vehicle to rid the world of tyranny and oppression. Exactly what the Muslim world needs right now and has continually needed. Muslims face tyranny, injustice and the very fundamental need to be accepted or granted equal status. We're fighting so many things at the same time. Constantly struggling with not being economically empowered to do the things we need to.

In its correct role, which is as a means to create change in society and to generate wealth, entrepreneurship becomes not only useful and important, but vitally imperative. Islam dictates that we establish ourselves as people that create change in society, that we establish justice and rid ourselves of oppression, tyranny, injustice.

Again Silicon Valley proves this very point. Let's talk about Uber.

In their very well and researched article, Priceonomics explains the dilemmatic state of the taxi industry in California before the arrival of Uber.

"During a shift, taxi drivers play a strange form of roulette when they pick up anonymous customers. The customer could be a pleasant family that tips them well, a drunk college kid that vomits in their car, or a violent criminal that robs and assaults them. After the customer leaves the car, there is no record of their behavior in the taxi.

Why is it that taxi drivers have to pay their companies for the privilege of doing a difficult and dangerous job? After all, when you show up to your office, you don't pay a fee to your boss every morning.

The reason taxi drivers have to pay for the right to work is that they need access to a taxi medallion to do their job. A medallion is a permit issued by the government that is required to drive a cab in most cities in America. If you don't use the medallion yourself, you can rent it out to other drivers on your own or, more commonly, through a taxi company. Taxi companies that rent out access to the medallions have immense economic power over the drivers. If you're not willing to basically become an indentured servant to get medallion access, well, you're out of luck.

Taxi medallions are scarce, which is what makes them powerful. It also makes them expensive; medallions sell for hundreds of thousands of dollars on secondary markets depending on the city. In most American cities, there is a hard cap on the number of permits issued. That number doesn't change for years or even decades. This scarcity of medallions is also the reason it's so hard to find a taxi in many American cities (cough cough, San Francisco)."

This medallion issued by the Government of California as a means of "regulation" became a platform of tyranny. This very form of regulation meant that for a very long time, society at large suffered incredibly poor customer service, taxis were often not available when most needed if, for example, a pregnant woman needed to get to the hospital, someone was late for a critical meeting and so on. There was a very real and costly impact on society.

That is until Uber came along.

Priceonomics' article "The Tyrrany of Taxi Medallions" summarizes the insane situation of the taxi industry before Uber pushed the industry's unrelenting and out-dated regulations:

"The current structure of the American taxi industry began in New York City when "taxi medallions" were introduced in the 1930s. Taxis were extremely popular in the city, and the government realized they needed to make sure drivers weren't psychopaths luring victims into their cars. So, New York City required cabbies to apply for a taxi medallion license. Given the technology available in the 1930s, it was a reasonable solution to the taxi safety problem, and other cities soon followed suit. (Many of them have different names for the licenses, but we'll refer to them all as medallions.)

But the taxi medallion requirement had an unintended consequence - it made taxis scarce. The "right" to drive a taxi become very valuable as demand outstripped supply. When this medallion system was introduced in New York City in 1937, there were 11,787 issued. That number remained constant until 2004. Today there are 13,150.

As demand for taxis has increased with supply relatively fixed, the cost of the medallion in New York City has skyrocketed to over a million dollars a year. Even after adjusting for inflation, taxi medallions prices are absurd."

New taxi drivers had a huge barrier to entry, and even when they wanted to, they couldn't help improve the state of customer service and experience for the market. The cost of entry was just too high. But then Uber realised a legitimate loophole in the regulation, and instead of directly employing taxi drivers, Uber offered the service as a ride sharing service where customers make a "donation". This opportunity opened the doors for taxi drivers to offer their services without the huge costs associated with medallions.

"The root cause of taxi drivers' problems is that they need access to a medallion in order to drive and make a living. Because of this, taxi companies that distribute medallion access can charge usurious fees and freely abuse the drivers. If the drivers don't like it, well, then they can't be taxi drivers then."

But, the power of entrepreneurs to question and re-define the status quo is captured clearly in a comment by Uber investor Ashton Kutcher: "You're not even actually taking on the taxi companies– you're taking on the notion of owning a car," says Kutcher. "That's crazy. And that's why it has the velocity and potential that it has" (Greenburg, Zach O'Malley. "How Ashton Kutcher and Guy Oseary Built A \$250 Million Portfolio with Startups Like Uber and Airbnb". Forbes. 19 Apr 2016).

And thus the Uber disruption economy started, and since then Uber has become the fastest growing local transport provider in the world, valued at over $18 billion and attracting investments from high profile CEOs such as Jeff Bezos (Amazon).

Not only did Uber generate a huge amount of wealth for itself and its partners (Uber taxi drivers are often part-time drivers that use it as a secondary means of living), but it has attracted significant debate and called existing regulations into question, not just in the US but around the world. It has exposed the tyranny of those that tried to maintain the status quo and has caused significant disruption to their tyrannical ways.

This is what it means to break the status quo, take the high roads towards positive change, and ascend to incredible heights when we understand the true potentials of entrepreneurship.

But Uber isn't where things start or end. Entrepreneurship has always opened doors to affect change.

When Jack Dorsey co-founded Twitter as a micro-blogging service, not even he could imagine what a fundamental role it would play in both the political unrest in Iran in 2009 and the Arab Spring of 2011.

But that's not to say that Entrepreneurship is the reserve on tech companies or tech disruption only, or even, for that matter, those that seek to do good in the world. Entrepreneurship is simply an agent of change in society, the outcome of which is entirely dependent on the moral compass of the entrepreneur. Technology – though often seen as a key driver – is merely a form of leverage (though not to be under-estimated to say the least).

There's probably no better example of how important the moral compass of the entrepreneur is and the stark contrasts in the kinds of seismic shifts it can create than that of the British and their foray into India. In the late 19th Century, the Lords at Westminster decided to trade with India. Big ships were built to trade things like cotton and tea, and little by little the East India Company established a small but significant presence in India. The British attracted local, impoverished talent by offering higher wages and better employee welfare than their native counterparts, thus creating a talent surge which - amongst other things, such as their entrepreneurial prowess - enabled the East India Company to thrive. Eventually the company became so big that it rivalled the size of a state, giving it a seat at the political table to exact its colonial hegemony, and the rest is history.

Things are no different today. Just look at which kind of firms have historically paid higher wages and which kind of institutions have paid the least. Hint: the tyrannical corporations provide huge employee benefits and welfare, while the Muslim institutions try to get by paying as little as possible. Sadly, they do not realize that a simple change in attitude and a willingness to invest more towards attracting quality talent could make all the difference.

When this "tool" of Entrepreneurship is in the wrong hands, much like a sharp weapon, it can be a force of evil. This potential power is all the more reason for good people to replace the bad. Unfortunately, even up to recent history, many shifts of enormous proportion resulting from entrepreneurial movements have been driven by greed. Instead of deposing tyranny, they have further reinforced it or replaced it with their own version.

For example, not long after World War II, the oil barons in the West used business and trade as a carving knife to divvy up the Middle East. They continue this practice today behind the guise of stirring up civil strife and causing conflict and out-right war.

The media also hasn't helped to project a positive image of entrepreneurship. By highlighting cases on both extreme ends of the spectrum, (i.e. the struggling entrepreneur constantly battling with economic cycles of feast and famine and at the other end, the wealthy entrepreneur that has arrived at his station through his insatiable appetite of lust and greed), the media has perpetuated the myth that entrepreneurship is harder than a full time job and that wealth can only be made by striking it big through some stroke of random luck or by choosing to be unethical.

Alhamdulillah for many of the sahabah, such as Abu Bakr, Umar, Uthman, AbdurRahman bin Awf, Talhah bin Ubaydallah, and others (may Allah be please with all of them) who recognized the power of trade and its advantages for bringing about positive change and spreading benefit to greater numbers of people. These sahabah used trade successfully, not only for their personal livelihood, but also as a means to take Islam to the rest of the world. Even after the sahabah passed away, trade was a primary vehicle by which the Muslims spread Islam to Northern and Eastern Africa, Indonesia and Malaysia, and even as far east as China.

***

It's worth noting the underestimated power and significance of the small business. Many think that a lot of jobs come from bigger firms, or that at least in the developing world 90% of jobs are created by large firms. The general assumption is that large firms drive the economy. In reality, most economies are propped up by small businesses.

In the U.K. for example, there are more than 250,000 small businesses that pay a high amount of tax and create a huge number of jobs. Job creation shouldn't be taken as the only or most accurate measure of how well the economy is doing anyway, but even if we were to use that metric for the purposes of this discussion, we would have to concur that small businesses create more jobs and pay more taxes to contribute to the economy than their larger business counterparts.

In his book Wealth of Nations", Adam Smith noted that a key component of a thriving economy was a country that encouraged entrepreneurship. Furthermore, looking at nations or regions with fast-growing or well-established economies such as Israel or the state of California, we discover that these economies are robust and have risen rapidly because the governments have fostered entrepreneurship. Most of the innovations that we see in such economies whether it be the IPhone, Google Maps, the internet or automated robots in the cotton fields is actually funded research by their governments or initiated by the military and then handed over to entrepreneurs to take it to the masses.

Business drives the economy.

But despite all of this, entrepreneurship, most especially in the Muslim household, is seen as an undignified pursuit.

Aftab, having never been to University nor having had a corporate job, was now on his third business, this time selling mayonnaise sachets to take-aways. In his first year of business, Aftab's mayonnaise company reached just over a million dollars in revenue. Aftab spent most of the first year driving business development and setting up distribution agreements. While there were many other facets of the business that needed to be taken care of, including driving down manufacturing and advertising costs, Aftab chose to defer this work to year two, anticipating that he wouldn't have to worry as much about doing the main ground work for sales and marketing. As part of this long-term decision however, it meant that Aftab's company only broke even in the first year. Still, a million dollars in revenue was worth shouting about, or at least, so he thought.

Being fairly active in the local Muslim community, Aftab started telling his friends about his business success. Eager to help other Muslims and seeing how it had changed his life, he decided to launch a course to help others get into entrepreneurship. Aftab reached out to a number of Islamic groups, both online and offline, and took an "Islamic" approach to inviting people to entrepreneurship. There was, however, a slight problem. Many of Aftab's friends who were considered to be more prominent members in society, practicing brothers with huge social media followings and known for their activism, started to question his integrity. They asked him how much profit he'd made in the first year, to which he answered he'd only broken even. And that's when all the trouble started. These influential brothers -- who often attended talks together, helped aid convoys, did charity work and, of course, socialized and spent their free time together -- suddenly started "warning" the community about a "fake entrepreneur" that was only out to "take their money". Things went even further, when in many of the community gatherings, these brothers would do quick satirical presentations mimicking Aftab's sales copy and then end by advising those listening to go get a job.

Disappointed by the conduct of these "influential" brothers, Aftab abandoned his dream to encourage more entrepreneurs in the community. His goal of 20 entrepreneurial founders by the end of the year, remained an unrealized dream, and quite ironically, one of the brothers who did the satirical presentation lost his job and remained unemployed for a number of months. Aftab went on in his own business to make a healthy profit in year two.

Unfortunately, this kind of ridicule for the "unsuccessful" entrepreneur in the Muslim community is very common. A "steady job" is seen as the holy grail of financial freedom, yet nothing could be further from the truth. Job security is only an illusion, not to mention the finite limit to one's earning potential.

Criticising someone for having tried entrepreneurship and failing to become an overnight success is no different from ridiculing someone that jumped on a bike for the first time and fell off. No one tells the first time biker to go back to walking, or points fingers at them for having the audacity to imagine themselves riding a bike. Yet when it comes to business, every non-entrepreneur thinks they're an expert and peddles the cliché that getting a job is the sensible and dignified thing to do.

Is it the position of the mu'min to abandon all forms of ambition and determination? When did we learn to not take risks in life? When ever did timidity and being overly cautious become a badge of honour?

It's as if to say that entrepreneurs are only worth talking to if they've reached society's existing definition of success, which is worldwide fame and owning millions in the bank. Until reaching that level, employ in a "secure" job is viewed a better and wiser option. The irony is that the failed entrepreneur is still closer to being a successful entrepreneur than the one in a full time job working for somebody else. It's a shame then, that this very fear of criticism from the community holds so many first time entrepreneurs back. Their courage to dream is so vigorously ridiculed and so brashly stifled that they never even bother trying to mount the entrepreneurial bike, let alone learn to ride it.

In the end, falling and getting back up again is an indispensable part of the learning process. And for the Muslim who believes in qadr, the inevitable failures are taken in stride with the promised successes. Azzam Sheikh of Digital Marketing ROI makes this point very clear:

A Muslim as an entrepreneur does not measure failure or success on money!

They have absolute conviction in Allah whereby whatever is written for them will come and whatever is not written for them will not come.

However, a Muslim entrepreneur has the qualities of passion, drive, tenacity, positive mindset, etc. which are funneled into their businesses that lead them to achieve phenomenal growth and success. But if they didn't, no problem; move on to the next. Failure and Success are all the same to them.

10 CHAPTER

THE CAMBRIDGE YEARS:
OPPORTUNITY IS ALL AROUND US

"When one door closes another opens. But often we look so long, so regretfully upon the closed door that we fail to see the one that has opened for us."

Helen Keller

As I sat in Mr. Harriman's information systems lecture a few weeks into the academic year, his announcement about internships caused mixed feelings of excitement and dread in me. On the one hand, I really wanted a chance to go into the 'real world', apply my skills, and earn. This would be my first real job, but on the other hand, I didn't want a job far from home. I wanted to continue living with my parents.

At the end of the lecture, I approached Mr. Harriman and asked him if there was any way I could ensure getting an internship in Sheffield (my home town). He told me it all depended on how good

62

my application was, what internships were available and how well I would interview. On my application there would be no way to indicate which regions I wanted to work in. Either I confirmed I wanted an internship and opened myself to the whole of the UK, or I skipped the year altogether. I didn't think it would be too difficult to secure a place in Sheffield. Sheffield had plenty of employers looking to take on interns. Or so I thought.

By the end of October, I had submitted all my internship applications and had heard nothing. Then I got a phone call from an excited careers lady telling me I had been selected for interview at a large corporate in Cambridge. My heart sank, Cambridge was 120 miles from my home town. To a naive and homely boy like me, it was the equivalent to the other side of the world. For all intents and purposes, it might as well have been in Timbuktu. However, I couldn't bring myself to say no to the careers lady, so asked her for the details of the interview and if there was anything else I needed to know. She told me there would be three other candidates applying for the same job, and two of us would be selected. By this point, I had made up my mind that I would skip the internship altogether. I was tired of working hard at the computer shop, and I felt I was missing out on my youth. My friends were out playing football every weekend and watching the Matrix, while I was at Mr. Geoffrey's house for the fifth time showing him how to use the new ink-jet printer he had purchased from us.

I knew it would look bad if I turned down the interview offer. My career supervisor and my school friends would be disappointed. So I hatched a plan. Given that the odds of me not securing a place were already quite high, I figured all I had to do was perform poorly at my interview. Then I could tell my careers supervisor that I wasn't good enough for the job, and mum wouldn't need to know I had a defeatist attitude. It was a good plan — in theory. I had my plan; my Lord had His.

The interview date arrived and as per my plan, my intent was to do a mediocre interview and leave it at that. Unfortunately for me, my prospective employers didn't judge my interview that way. They read my dispassion as confidence, and since I had built over a thousand PCs by this time, my experience naturally shone through. They were impressed, and within 24hrs I received confirmation that I had got the position.

I kept looking for an opportunity to turn down the job; even as I walked into the careers office, accepted congrats from Mr. Harriman, the careers lady and my friends, and signed the internship forms, I was still searching for any excuse I could offer. But the ball had already started rolling, and before I knew it I had already found a place to stay in Cambridge, bought some new work shirts, got a car (Thanks Dad) and was on my way to moving in.

My whole body was consumed in dread.

Work on the first day began with Nigel as my supervisor. I was introduced to the other interns from the previous year who still had another six months left on their internship. They seemed a very friendly and eager bunch.

Ranbir was assigned to mentoring me for the first couple of weeks so that I could learn the company procedures, policies and my way around the business park which had more than six buildings and was probably a couple of square miles in size.

I don't remember much of the first day, but I do remember that Ranbir and I hit it off from day one. I really enjoyed spending my work time with him. The rest of the staff in the IT department, all seemed very friendly and especially helpful, and the work itself wasn't particularly difficult. It was challenging, but in a good way. I'd always wanted to work in a corporate environment and see how IT is used in the enterprise, so this was a chance to improve my skills and get some really good experience. I couldn't wait to see my parents and little sister though.

On the way home from work after the first day, as darkness fell on to the main dual carriageway en route, I calculated how many times I'd have to drive over on this road over the coming year, but before I could come up with the answer, I realised I had another whole year to go; I was alone, in Cambridge — without my parents. I was hating it already. One year in a 19-year old's life is a long time. The thought looming in my mind was as dark, cold and overcast as the scene developing over the carriageway.

Odd then, I now tell people it was probably the greatest year of my life. That year I made Hajj. It was a journey that ignited my on-going interest in the deen, alhumdulillah. I discovered the gym, had great trips to London and many other memorable experiences.

By the time I finished my placement, as much as I wanted to be closer to my parents, a huge part of me didn't want to go back home. My year in Cambridge had been incredible. I was sad a pivotal year was coming to an end.

I entered the year in Cambridge with dread and left it with more experience and fond memories. It is truly amazing how Allah shows us the goodness and value in something over time. Our mistake is approaching such things with nothing but voices of complaint and lack of gratitude, just as I did when my year there started.

Ibn Qayyim al-Jawziyyah said it most eloquently: "Had Allah lifted the veil for His slave and shown him how He handles his affairs for him, and how Allah is more keen for the benefit of the slave than his own self, his heart would have melted out of the love of Allah and would have been torn to pieces out of thankfulness to Allah".

The whole time I was in Cambridge, all I could think about was how my family was 120 miles away, how I had no friends in Cambridge, how there were no other Muslims for me to meet, and how there was nothing for me to do. This mindset of focusing on what was missing, instead of what there was, was what caused me to miss out on other opportunities and experiences. I now regret how little of Cambridge I explored that year. All because I spent a large part of the year feeling like I shouldn't have been in Cambridge in the first place.

Now, more than 15 years later, despite the fact that I had a great year, I realise I didn't give enough thanks for the opportunity I had been given by Allah.

Ever since I've been married I've been telling my wife of

anecdotes here and there relating to Cambridge and how much I enjoyed my time there. We talked about taking a day trip from London one sunny day. So recently, that sunny day and opportunity arrived. I drove us into Cambridge and looked for the business park, and then the house where I had lived. On the way in, I took a wrong turn about a mile from the house and ended up at the University. It was no more than ten minutes by car from where I actually wanted to be, but I hadn't explored this part of Cambridge before. I had driven past it on the odd occasion but never stepped out to take a look. My wife was taken in by the surroundings, and the general ambience of the area, so she suggested we stop, explore the area and go look for the house later.

We arrived around 11 a.m. at the University area and didn't leave till around 4 p.m. We took a walk by the river and explored the University buildings. My wife admired the architecture, and then we took a stroll around the shops leading up to the city centre. It was an incredibly enjoyable day. But what really amazed my wife was that each area we explored was as new to me as it was to her. This was a part of Cambridge I hadn't visited or explored before despite it being literally ten minutes down the road from where I had lived during my time there. In the 12 months I lived in Cambridge, I only stayed there for one weekend. Though the year was filled with plenty of great experiences in terms of my time away, my experiences at work, and learning about independence, all I could ever think about while I was there was seeing my cousins, seeing my parents, and getting as much time in my hometown as possible. I would leave Cambridge as early as possible on Friday evenings and return back to Cambridge as late as possible, so I could make the most of my time back home with my family.

I never once stopped to see what Cambridge itself had to offer, and as it turns out, Cambridge has a lot to offer students. This was an opportunity I had missed.

We spend our whole lives focusing on what's missing from our lives, what we don't have enough of, or waiting for conditions to conform to our ideals before taking action. If there's anything that I learned from the Cambridge experience, it's that such a mindset stems from a lack of gratitude. Not being thankful for what we already have limits our ability to benefit from even more goodness. It constrains us into a mindset that blinds us to the opportunities that are all around us. Resisting the opportunity to immerse ourselves in new experiences wastes the opportunity that presents itself right before us.

A little bit of discomfort in the short-term can open up a whole world of possibilities and amazing experiences in the long term. I remember one sister once told me that she had never learned to drive her car outside of her home town. She often found the experience too daunting, but now that her own daughter was of driving age, she was able to enjoy all the sights of the nature reserves and elegant British towns in the nearby city — all in a day trip. Something this sister herself had not allowed herself to do. Now, she says, out of fear of having to memorise and learn new routes at the time (over 20 years ago!) she missed out on many wonderful sightseeing experiences. Memories she could have made for her two daughters and great times she could have had. She spent many weekends waiting for her husband to come home from his weekend shifts to be able to visit the nearby places, only to find that he was often exhausted from work or he would come home quite late, leaving little time to take full advantage of the excursion. All because she resisted stepping out of her comfort zone.

***

I once had a conversation with a brother about the success of a billionaire. The brother told me that he didn't want to hear any more of this other person's success because he felt that the only reason this entrepreneur was successful was because he had come from a privileged background. While that may have been true, I failed to get the brother to see that in real terms that didn't make much difference. Just because the entrepreneur may have been able to start off with an extra $50-100 thousand than the rest of us, didn't mean that we were more deprived of opportunity than he was. In fact, a couple of months earlier a mutual friend had raised just over $750 thousand through crowd-sourcing. A far higher number than what the billionaire started with. This kind of attitude stems from what many call the "Elephant and the Rope mentality":

"As a man was passing a group of elephants in a circus, he

suddenly stopped, confused by the fact that these huge creatures were being held by only a small rope tied to their front leg. No chains, no cages. It was obvious that the elephants could, at any time, break away from their bonds but for some reason, they did not.

He saw a trainer nearby and asked why these animals just stood there and made no attempt to get away. "Well," trainer said, "when they are very young and much smaller we use the same size rope to tie them and, at that age, it's enough to hold them. As they grew up, they are conditioned to believe they cannot break away. They believe the rope can still hold them, so they never try to break free."

The man was amazed. These animals could at any time break free from their bonds but because they believed they couldn't, they were stuck right where they were."

It is for this reason that many don't choose entrepreneurship. The fear of the unknown often takes us out of our comfort zone. We resist with 'excuses' that we don't have a good enough "idea", or we don't have "enough" money, or market conditions are not "conducive" to business, or that others are more privileged than us. Yet some of the best businesses started as simple ideas, with founders that had little to no money who were also facing economic recessions. Records have it that, the period between 1929-1931 created the largest number of millionaires in history. It was the time that most remember as "The Great Depression". Instead of focusing on what was missing those millionaires chose to focus on what was possible.

Getting prepared and doing an appropriate amount of planning is critical in most undertakings, but most of the time, procrastinating due to lack of apparent opportunity is nothing but an excuse. What we have in the present is an opportunity to be grateful, and the unknown is an opportunity to learn something new and to experience greater possibilities.

11 CHAPTER

OPERATING IN TRUTH
CONFORMING IS FOR WIMPS

"People may hate you for being different and not living by society's standards, but deep down they wish they had the courage to do the same."

Kevin Hart

In the summer of 1893, a young Italian man, not yet twenty, shared a conjecture about physics with friends. He believed it was possible for man to transmit signals wirelessly. His well-intended friends showed some cause for alarm. After all, how could data be transmitted just through "thin air"?

The thought was as preposterous as suggesting cats can fly.

Thus, with all good intentions, they did what they thought best and referred him to a mental institution. In the summer of 1895, this same man successfully transmitted a wireless signal containing audio data, at a distance of 2.4km. By 1909, Guglielmo Marconi -- credited as the inventor of radio -- was awarded a Nobel Prize in Physics for his contribution to Radio communication.

Marconi acted on his own truth and changed the world forever.

***

At twenty years old, a truck driver in California named James taught himself about special effects:

"I'd go down to the USC library and pull any thesis that graduate students had written about optical printing, or front screen projection, or dye transfers, anything that related to film technology. That way I could sit down and read it, and if they'd let me photocopy it, I would. If not, I'd make notes."

After seeing the original Star Wars film in 1977, this truck driver quit his job to enter the film industry. When he read Syd Field's book Screenplay, it occurred to him that integrating science and art was possible. He wrote a 10-minute science-fiction script with two friends, titled Xenogenesis. They raised some money and rented a camera, lenses, film stock and studio and then shot it in 35mm. They dismantled the camera to understand how to operate it and spent the first half-day of the shoot trying to figure out how to get it running.

James was the director, writer, producer, and production designer for Xenogenesis (1978). He then became an uncredited production assistant on a film called Rock and Roll High School in 1979. While continuing to educate himself in film-making techniques, James started working as a miniature-model maker at Roger Corman Studios. Making rapidly produced, low-budget productions taught

James to work efficiently and effectively. He soon found employment as an art director in the sci-fi movie Battle Beyond the Stars (1980). After a series of minor special effect roles, he was hired as the special effects director of a low budget sequel. After some creative differences, the original director left the movie and James was given the chance to direct his first film.

The sequel (with a 7% approval rating on rotten tomatoes) is considered, by some, one of the worst films of all time. However, its then unaccomplished director is now considered one of the greatest sci-fi film-makers in modern film history. His name is James Cameron, and he was the director of blockbusters such as Terminator II and Titanic.

In his own words:

"I spent just $120 on my film making education and then went on to direct Terminator II ..... eventually".

James knew his truth and followed it. He didn't let anyone tell him he couldn't enter the world of film-making without a formal education in the subject or formal work experience.

***

The question on Haseeb's mind was always: "If all that matters is earning a living and being able to take care of one's parents, then why does it have to be done via dentistry"?

Haseeb was an average student in high school. He didn't do particularly well in his exams, most probably because his mind was always on what kind of a business he'd like to run when he finished school. His parents though, like most Indian parents, had high hopes for his dentistry career instead. Haseeb's father was a shopkeeper whose workday started at 6 a.m. and ended at 12 a.m., six days a week.

After high school, when it came to choosing his career, Haseeb felt he had to choose dentistry owing the decision almost entirely to his parents' ambitions and desires for their eldest son. On weekends, while the few friends he had from the University would be in the library reading "New Scientist", Haseeb was scouring European distributor websites for sourcing Nike and Reebok trainers.

Just before exam week started for the first academic year, Haseeb placed an order for 20 pairs of Nike Air running shoes to be delivered to his student flat. In four years of trying, this was now his sixth attempt at finding a product he could sell for a reasonable profit on eBay. He'd tried: coffee tables, teddy bears, jewelry and boxing gloves; all of which had lost him money. But this time, he had a hunch. He figured the shipment would arrive by the time he finished his last exam and then he could spend a couple weeks of the summer vacation selling the items on eBay and Amazon before he headed back home to his parents. Unfortunately, the shipment never arrived that weekend.

Haseeb's debit card was registered at his parents' house, and since this was a first time order, the distributor could only ship to the verified debit card address. His parents were surprised at the arrival of the shipment which filled their main hallway with boxes, and they were incredibly disappointed by their son's obvious lack of commitment to his studies and his zealous commitment to selling running shoes.

A few months later, down to the last pair of sports shoes and having sold most of the pairs on eBay with some difficulty, Haseeb looked back on his summer. He couldn't help but wonder, why, if there was such demand for Nike trainers, that his shoes weren't selling so well. He started looking through similar sales items from others, and before he knew it, he'd spent over six hours carefully analysing every Nike Air item listing from other eBay power sellers. He had spotted a pattern. The other sellers, though charging slightly higher prices, were going to great lengths to make sure they had good product shots, 100% feedback and a very good quality description.

Haseeb didn't have the best feedback so far, as he had a number of his shipments that went out later than he had promised. In addition, he always assumed he'd have to compete on price, and never paid attention to his item descriptions. Alas, it was now too late to do anything about, but just for fun and for the sake of satisfying his curiosity, he decided to apply his observations to his last sale listing.

The shoes sold within a few hours. Haseeb was onto something just as his exam results came through the post. Haseeb had failed two out of the five exams. He would now have to re-sit.

Of course, his father was deeply disappointed. Haseeb was given an ultimatum that night, either he would get his "act together" by getting his head down to study, or he would be expected to take over his father's duties at the shop and would be taken back to India the following summer, where he'd be expected to get married. Both options were equally unappealing to Haseeb.

Again, Haseeb thought: If the bills for the house were being paid and his father no longer worked, then as long as the income was halal, what difference did it make if the money was coming from cleaning people's teeth or from shipping a few hundred boxes of trainers from home.

In September, Haseeb headed back to dentistry school. Payment had already been made on his rent for the next six months, so Haseeb decided to take advantage of it. However, he had no intention of re-sitting his exams. Instead he enrolled for a call centre job with a new mobile operator that had been making waves in the press. They had excelled in their reputation for good customer service. Haseeb spent the next three months working at the call centre four days on and four days off. In his time off, he would buy more trainers, sell the stock on eBay and then re-invest his tidy little sums of profit. By now, he'd gotten so good with his listing descriptions that he could afford to experiment with higher margin goods.

These days Haseeb has moved into selling Kitchen appliances and has one of the most popular stores on eBay. He has seven staff members and a warehouse not far from his parents' home. His father sold the shop one year after Haseeb returned from his last year at dentist school and spends most days reading the paper, meeting his other shopkeeper buddies in the evening at the masjid, and spending time with Haseeb's mother. Haseeb pays for the house bills. He also paid for the kitchen extension and supplied the new kitchen appliances, of course. He is currently saving money to pay for his little sister's wedding.

His father isn't quite ready to convince his other shopkeeper friends to let their sons make their own career choices just yet, but suffice to say, he's no longer pushing his son to become a dentist.

Haseeb allowed his intuition to guide him. Today, things couldn't be better.

***

When Zaira suggested the idea of a virtual assistant to her colleagues at the local non-profit, her suggestion was met with some nervous laughs. One sister replied to the suggestion by saying, "We're not Richard Branson you know. He can afford to have two personal assistants on their MacBook's typing up his emails while sitting by the pool. But that's because he's a billionaire. We don't have that luxury, nor are we that posh. And besides we want the reward of helping these girls for ourselves".

Zaira, a project manager at a Pharmaceutical company listed on the FTSE 500 spent the first year of her new job assigning all her immediate delegates to reading the drug research papers and reports as well as personally preparing all client reports. Two months into the start of the new year, with approval from her line manager and access to surplus company funds, Zaira hired a team of virtual assistants from the Philippines. For the price of one team member in-house, she could hire four part-time virtual assistants on a contract basis. Four months into the outsourcing arrangement, Zaira's department had exceeded revenue targets by more than 300%. Her line manager wanted to know what it was her team was doing that was making this possible. Zaira attributed it to her team's ability to be able to process more sales related administration (thanks to the VAs) which therefore meant capacity to take on more clients.

Zaira shared her insights with the other departments over the next 12 months. This year the company posted its highest sales revenues for the last decade, and Zaira had a lot to do with it.

Thinking about how following her gut instinct had helped her at work, Zaira was keen to replicate the same with the local non-profit she helped on evenings and weekends. Zaira was part of a team of professional sisters that had banded together to provide career support to young Muslim girls who needed help with their career development. The sisters had been running the non-profit off the back of their own personal funds. The sisters would help the young girls with their applications for universities and job searches. The beneficiaries loved the help and guidance, and within twelve months of opening the non-profit had helped five girls choose a fitting career path, and had them all placed at their chosen universities. They even helped them find accommodation.

Zaira and her colleagues took immense satisfaction from helping the young girls, but after a year passed, they realised how financially and practically demanding the work was.

The taxing nature of the work took its toll, and the amount of energy each person could dedicate to the non-profit was decreasing which subsequently meant so was the quality, which in turn meant fewer girls were being placed at university. But Zaira didn't want to give up on the non-profit. She thought again about the option of contracting VA's for the non-profit. She was left with a single question: 'Why not?' .

"But that's the point." said Zaira. "It's not about being posh, or corporate. Personal assistants aren't expensive anyway". Her colleagues wouldn't have any of it, but as luck would have it, each sister resigned from her duties one after the other due to a myriad of personal and extenuating circumstances. In the end, the only person left was Zaira.

Since the leaving sisters were still donating funds, Zaira decided to use this money to hire VAs for the non-profit. Within just three weeks, Zaira's virtual assistant team had gone from being able to help five girls each week to 16 girls each week, all of this without creating any more work for Zaira.

Now Zaira could focus on more strategic matters. So, she

decided to set-up a system that once each girl had been successfully placed at university, she was now to help three other girls at the café until they had been placed. If she did this, she would be entitled to free interview preparation and practise when it came to time for applying for real world jobs. This was a win-win. Around a third of the girls signed up for this offer which meant that Zaira only had to make an appearance for around 30 minutes once a week and make sure that all was OK. The rest of the non-profit's operations were taken care of by the VAs and the girls themselves. Now, the non-profit attends to around 30 girls each week. Zaira would love for other sisters to adopt such a model up and down the country, but sadly that reality hasn't taken place just yet.

Zaira knew her truth and by acting on her gut instincts she multiplied the non-profit's effectiveness and proficiency; instead of being able to help just five girls a year, the non-profit can now help more than thirty.

***

Western society has a strange way of luring us away from recognising our own truths and acting upon them. Instead of allowing our intuition to guide us, we choose to rely purely on intellect to lead our way. Incidentally, this is one of the first observations that Steve Jobs made when he returned from a long stint in India.

"Coming back to America was, for me, much more of a cultural shock than going to India. The people in the Indian countryside don't use their intellect like we do; they use their intuition instead, and their intuition is far more developed than in the rest of the world. Intuition is a very powerful thing, more powerful than intellect in my opinion. That's had a big impact on my work" -- Steve Jobs. Late founder of Apple

We're a series of nations that have trained ourselves to look for answers in spreadsheets, textbooks, academic papers and bar charts, yet a world of answers awaits us right in our own solar plexus.

Operating in truth liberates us from being prisoners of our own minds or of society's expectations. Not only do we need to operate in truth, but we need to stop others from imposing their truths on us as well. Of course, we need to differentiate between what exactly our truth is and what delusions of grandeur are. The former will push us in the right direction to realise our full potential, while the latter should be avoided.

Chris Gardner, an entrepreneur who went from homelessness to self-made success is emphatic upon this point: "Don't let anyone tell you, you can't do something. Not even me. You have a dream; you got to protect it. [When] people can't do something themselves, they [want to] tell you, you can't do it either. You want something. Go get it. Period!" (Pursuit of Happyness).

The ultimate key to achieving our goals is to understand our own truth. It's only then that we can create the life that we desire. What people like Haseeb and Zaira did is stop listening to other people's voices, i.e. the "truths" of others and the "truths" of society. Instead, they listened to their own inner voice. They became clear about what they wanted and their own sense of purpose and committed to living it. They allowed their intuition to guide them in living that truth and making decisions to realise their true sense of purpose. This is known as operating in truth, and it is the ultimate key to success and happiness. Instead of focusing on what we think we should do, we need to focus on what we want to do. The more we tune into our intuition and the more we listen to it, the better we will get at achieving our goals, attaining contentment and finding happiness. The mind is an incredible tool for computing things, but it is incredibly poor at good judgement and decision making. Our intuition is far better equipped for that.

There will always be "noise" and other voices that distract us from what our intuition tells us. There will always be those that impose their own truths upon us and suppress our instincts, but the real test is to live our truth despite those distractions and impositions. That is the difference between those that live their full potential and those that don't. That is the difference between those that live the life they want and those that don't.

"Operating in truth is being honest with yourself. Being

77

vulnerable with your own self and letting deep down issues bubble to the surface to be dealt with. Because most people are just suppressing these issues because of societal pressures, parental pressures, peer pressure - or whatever it might be - especially in the Muslim community where we have so many expectations of our kids, like becoming doctors and lawyers and so on. They're expected to become pharmacists, open a pharmacy, get married and then have six children and then live life on auto-pilot until they pass away. It's such a mundane, boring, meaningless and impactless life. It's not a meaningful existence. Not in the slightest. Absolutely none." -- Ramiz Ali

12 CHAPTER

OUR GREATEST HANDICAP:
IT'S NOT LACK OF TALENT, IDEAS OR
INTELLIGENCE

*"I removed your ego, and it turns out that's what was clogging up
your perception of reality."*

Someecards.com

A father-son duo started a computer shop business around the time of the dotcom era, prior to the e-commerce boom. The son, who had previous computer assembly and technical experience, taught the staff how to build PC's. He set up the invoicing and accounting system and established positive relationships with the suppliers. The father focused on more legal, financial and administrative matters. He set up the limited company, invested money into inventory and took responsibility for hiring and firing. The son was the resident technician and operations person, while the father was the business manager.

In the first year of business, this new business reached just under $1.5 million in operating revenues. An impressive figure for a small computer shop with just a few staff.

More and more people purchased computer modems to get connected to the internet at home, and broadband had finally started to become a reality. Though the adoption of high-speed internet was still pretty slow, and Amazon was still largely focusing on book sales, it had become obvious that the future was in e-commerce. eBay was largely still just a U.S. phenomenon, and most companies barely had a website, let alone the ability to sell from their website. Still, it was readily obvious to the son that it was just a matter of time before things reached a tipping point.

The son insisted, since the company had a surplus of cash, to make investments for the long term by focusing all the company's energies on e-commerce. The father was more interested in keeping the things the way they were. Business was doing well, and he saw no reason to change course. Changing course for e-commerce would mean the company would have to focus on volume with lower margins, since online selling had sizeable associated transaction fees, while their current business model was geared towards higher margins per transaction.

As the son tried to convince his father of the huge opportunity ahead and how the company needed to move fast to capitalise on it, the father said to his son: "You have to learn to walk before you can run"

Just five years later, Amazon moved into selling electronics; eBay had become a global phenomenon, and scores of e-commerce stores selling computer items and accessories were now competing to take advantage of the growing online market. The small computer shop was now drowning amongst the intense competition from the online stores that shipped greater volume at lower prices.

Now the company is a shadow of its former self. The golden opportunity had passed, and the surplus of cash is gone.

***

One man, not far from Silicon Valley in the U.S., came up with a "revolutionary" e-commerce idea. E-commerce was already big business, but he felt his idea was something that could make the market even more interesting and potent.

With great belief in his revolutionary idea, he arranged a number of meetings with VC funds and Angel investors. Since he was so confident his idea was going to change the world, he insisted every meeting participant sign an NDA (non-disclosure agreement) before he revealed the idea. His friends and family knew he was working on something big, but he didn't share his idea with even them. Everyone knew James was working on something big, it was the talk around town, but no one knew what the big idea was.

A number of angel investors expressed provisional interest in James' idea, but wanted to see a working product before they could make an actual decision to invest. At this point, all James had was just an idea. He had no prototype or actual product.

James quit his well-paying IT job, re-mortgaged his house (against his wife's will), used the extra equity to hire two full time developers and began work on building the product. The team spent approximately three times as long as most teams would, delayed by choosing the right technology for building the product. James was insistent that since this idea was going to be so big, the technology choice had to be right from the get-go. Both developers also had to sign an NDA, and they were instructed not to discuss the product with their friends or their families. They were told in no uncertain terms that if anyone outside of the team was to get even a sneak at what the product looked like, they would be fired instantly, no questions asked.

When the feature specification of the software was reviewed and discussed, the developers insisted that building out all the features would take too long and that it would be better to release an early beta version with limited features to gain traction. They advised that this initial step would help generate a modicum of revenue, make it easier to attract investment, and ultimately allow them to focus on building out the fuller product to take advantage of the larger opportunity ahead.

But James balked and said to his developers: "I can understand that other companies are working this way but this idea is too special for me to take the risk of releasing it into the market too early. So just carry on programming."

Twelve months later, James ran out of money. The product was never finished, and the technology landscape changed drastically rendering most of the development work irrelevant.

James' big idea was shelved, along with his marriage.

***

A young man in his late twenties, whose father had recently passed away, inherited a sizeable amount of wealth. David, not having worked a day in his life, decided to start a web development/marketing agency. Within a few months of starting, David secured a corporate client and was tasked with developing their website for their new business launch.

David hired a team twice the size needed, organised a major launch party and rented a three-storey office block. The team members all questioned the necessity of the office building when they could all fit into one room on the first floor. If the first floor itself was excessive space, then three floors was simply insane.

As work began on the new website, the team insisted that the terms of the contract were flawed, and that the website development, technology choice and task distribution were inefficient. One particular team member, considered by his peers to be the most experienced, was a little more vocal than the rest of the team. David had a special lunchtime meeting with him and told him that he felt he had a "chip on his shoulder". He also withheld this team member's first week's salary payment due to his 'opinionated' approach to work.

Worried for his job, the experienced team member decided to relent and continued his work in silent protest. There was a growing sentiment of anxiety amongst the team however. Many bits of work were often scrapped, re-done and sometimes just impossible. The team was worried that despite all this frustration and anxiety, there remained a high probability that the client would be disappointed with the end result and refuse to pay. But David insisted he knew better and told them to continue.

During this same time-frame, David was busy jet-setting around Europe and the U.S., skiing the slopes, playing tennis, sipping Pina Coladas on the beach and attending high-profile business conferences. At most business events, he insinuated to many that he was going to be on the next "30 under 30" CEO list. This was a list of 30 exceptional entrepreneurs under 30 years of age that was compiled by a major business magazine each year. David was confident his name would be on the list that year.

In the meantime, his team took the brunt of his disastrous operating decisions. Tears were so common that by now even some of the boys had had a cry to themselves.

After a rather lengthy period of jet-setting, David returned to the office. To his surprise, he found the project was yet unfinished. He decided to "crack a whip" on the team, by making them work late nights over Christmas and New Year to get the project finished. Christina missed dinner on Christmas eve with her mum; Ken received calls from David on Christmas morning with new tasks to be completed before the New Year, and Leonard missed quality time with his newborn daughter.

Five months later, the project that was supposed to take four weeks was still in progress, the client was beyond exasperated, most team members had left and the company was down five-figures in the bank.

***

A former senior developer at a major global tech firm decided to branch out on his own and start his own IT company. He partnered up with a less experienced co-founder, and they began providing IT support services to small businesses in the city.

After several years of arguing between himself and the other co-founder, Wayne insisted that he become the leader of the company and that his (less experienced) co-founder Kevin and the rest of the staff follow his "lead". Otherwise, in his words, "the company will never flourish". Tired of arguing, the co-founder relented and ceded operating control of the company.

Now in his role as leader, Wayne spent two full years getting the staff to build an all-singing, all-dancing customer management and business intelligence system, all the while refusing to take on any new business, prioritising existing customers and submitting accounts and legal work to the tax and governmental authorities.

However, Kevin insisted that the company should focus on serving existing customers and bringing in new business in parallel to developing the system. He further added that they should leverage pre-existing customer management and business intelligence systems in the market place rather than building their own, so they could focus on generating revenue. Wayne's response to Kevin was "You don't know anything about business. Creating a £1 million business requires great systems. We can't relegate this control to someone else. You need to have more faith in what I am doing. This is an essential part of being a follower. So just do your job."

By the third year, there was no change in the modus operandi, and the revenue from existing clients had halved, Kevin was gone, the customer management/business intelligence system suffered security breaches and the tax authorities issued a penalty that equalled around 20% of the company's annual turnover for failing to file the appropriate documents and records on time.

**

Faisal reminds us of the case of the Wright brothers versus Langley.

"Their [the Wright Brothers'] rival, a guy called Langley was Harvard educated, had millions of dollars of government funding, a huge team of engineers and the best minds to create the first flying machine, and yet, the Wright brothers were successful despite their lack of education and funding."

Arrogance harms trust, demoralises others and destroys the very essence of creativity in people. Creativity is requisite for innovation, so much so that creativity can be likened to the kindling of a fire.

In a well-known lecture, Nouman Ali Khan explains that those with an ego are usually the first to point out arrogance in others. The brutal irony is that people with an ego are so obsessed with the shortcomings and faults of others that they fail to see their own shortcomings.

In fact, if you're reading this, and the first thing you think of is other people that have an ego, then you most probably have an ego yourself.

In 1999, David Dunning and Justin Kruger published a study in the Journal of Personality and Social Psychology entitled "Unskilled and Unaware of It: How Difficulties in Recognizing One's Own Incompetence Lead to Inflated Self-Assessments". In this study, they posited the existence of what is now known as the "Dunning-Kruger Effect". In short it can be defined as a "cognitive bias wherein unskilled individuals suffer from illusory superiority, mistakenly assessing their ability to be much higher than is accurate." They further suggested that this bias forms because the "miscalibration of the incompetent stems from an error about the self, whereas the miscalibration of the highly competent stems from an error about others".

Great execution is rooted in the very essence of good decision making, but like a ship that sails slightly off course, the destructive nature of an ego is hardly ever immediately or readily apparent until it's too late.

In a world of increasing choice and disposable incomes, where the success of a company is less dependent on the customer's purse and more so on how she feels about the company, founders and leaders need to learn to look past their own noses. Many a company has withered embarrassingly due to the leader's insistence on paying no more than lip service to his team and his customer. Listening isn't just about hearing; it's about understanding.

People often cite the (possibly) mis-attributed quote of Henry Ford to counter argue the point: "If I'd asked people what they wanted, they would have asked for a faster horse."

While the sentiment may be true, the reality is that coming up with the idea of a motor vehicle that can get people to their destination faster and more reliably is heavily dependent on a deep rooted insight into the customer's psyche. Those with a penchant for deep empathy will realise, that what people were really saying was that they wanted to get to their destinations faster. This kind of remarkable insight, can never come from someone that insists on never getting out of their "own head".

But egos don't just present themselves through narcissism, they also have a monopoly on self-esteem.

Those that rationalise their insistence on hiding their works from others until it's "perfect", refrain from delegating decisive control or trust to others because it's too "risky", or resist any kind of criticism because it's "hurtful" are often acting out of a fear of vulnerability. This is a clear manifestation of low self-esteem. Such people guard their vulnerability so heavily that they're never able to commit wholesale to world-changing ideas, and neither do they have the courage to pursue their greatest ambitions.

Equally problematic is the fact that those with low self-esteem are often intent on bringing down others too; the mentality "If I won't do it, then I'll make sure you won't do it either" is rampant among those with low self-esteem. Those acting according to this mentality are nothing short of the person who ties a rock to the ankle of another and then pushes that other into deep water or like the one who pulls down on the swimmer that is trying to rise above the surface of the water (also known as leg-pulling).

When my aunt came to visit us in the UK from her home country of Pakistan, she once jokingly said to me that: "If 'leg-pulling' were an official sport, Pakistan would surely win at the Olympics".

Unfortunately, leg-pulling isn't a popular sport just in Pakistan. It's rampant in most societies, but often manifests itself in subtly different ways.

Unlike with narcissism (the ship that sails off course), the ship of low self-esteem never undocks or, if it does, never travels more than a few knots, let alone reach its destination.

May Allah Subhana wa ta'ala protect us from having over-inflated egos and from low self-esteem. Ameen.

13 CHAPTER

THE POWER OF INTENTION:
EVERYTHING STARTS WITH INTENTION

"We have come to know that thinking is a spiritual process, that vision and imagination precede action and event – that the day of the dreamer has come."

Charles F. Haanel

Several years ago, a friend of mine was forced, at the eleventh hour, to cancel plans to travel to Italy with me during my summer vacation. Despite the unfortunate occurrence, I was determined to take full advantage of my vacation allowance as I wouldn't get vacation again for another six months. I had no idea where I was going to go or what I was going to do, but I was determined to make it the best vacation I ever had. I had a shoestring budget that seemed to limit my options, but just six weeks later I was driving around a famous racing circuit in Europe in a high-end Porsche exceeding top speeds of 140mph. I had the time of my life. I didn't let my limited budget dictate boundaries; instead I put my intentions and determination forward to push me forward and open doors that I could have assumed to be locked.

A few years prior to that, at the turn of the millennium, I read an article in the national paper about outsourcing software development to the Indo-Pak region to reduce software development costs. Just nine weeks later, I flew to Pakistan, met the information minister in Karachi, rented an office and had two software developers working for me full-time. I would take software development orders from clients in my home town and then pass the orders onto my developers 8000 miles away in another country. Being a recent graduate, I had organised all this on a seemingly inadequate budget.

One day at my parent's house as I was taking a nap, I heard my sister call my name from downstairs. She was clearly in distress, but as I was only half awake, my brain interpreted it to be a dream. But her voice got louder and louder, and then she burst into my room frantically motioning to me to get to the kitchen as fast as possible. She was so panicked that she was unable to tell me the emergency. I approached the kitchen and noticed a bright light reflecting into the hallway from the kitchen. At first, I imagined that perhaps my mum wanted to share a new contraption or gadget but then immediately feared the worst. A fire had broken out in the kitchen. My mum's pressure cooker had turned into a huge ball of fire. The house was full of smoke, and the fire seemed it would spread fast if it wasn't dealt with immediately. I was deeply worried for the safety of my mum and two sisters.

This was a very serious and life-threatening situation. My sister was upstairs, and the fire was spreading fast. Being the only man in the house at the time, the responsibility of the situation fell on me the greatest. With no experience in fire-fighting, I foolishly tried to put out the fire by hitting the pressure cooker with a towel. As the big ball of fire fell to the floor and started to spread over the kitchen mat, I quickly realised my error and panicked even more. I urged my youngest sister to call the fire services while I desperately tried different approaches to resolve the situation.

I've always been afraid of fire. When I was still in primary school, two girls in a nearby town had died in a fire that broke out in their house at night while they were sleeping. We knew the family, and it devastated us all.

As my mum watched me struggling with varying strategies and the flames from the fire continuing to get bigger, my mum began to shout that I should leave the fire and just get out of the house. In her view, it wasn't worth trying to wrestle with the impending danger and risking our lives. But I knew the devastation to the kitchen and home would deeply affect her. My love for my mother pushed my resolve over the edge; I was determined to take charge and deal with the situation. I was going to extinguish that fire one way or another. I shouted for my mum to open the kitchen door, wrapped the mat around the ball of fire, picked it up (huge ball of fire and all) and then rushed out onto the patio and put it down on the floor. I had prepared myself mentally to run immediately to the garden and roll on the floor to extinguish any flames that might have caught on my clothes. I was expecting pain any second. I held my breath, looked down at my clothes, and to my surprise, there were no flames on me. Preparing myself for the worst, I turned around to check the kitchen. Maybe the flames hadn't caught me but had lit on something else in the kitchen. Again, I felt amazing relief! Not only had Allah protected me from the burning fire, but the flames hadn't caught anything else as I took the mat out. We watched as the flames petered out and released audible sighs of relief.

The emergency fire crew arrived just a few minutes later. Upon hearing about the situation and how I dealt with it, one of the fire professionals asked me if I had received former fire training. I replied honestly: "No, in fact, I am very afraid of dealing with fire, but I recalled some home videos I had seen on YouTube and tried to make the best of it." The fireman looked at me in amazement and told me that although my first attempt was very poor, my second attempt was excellent. He told us that most fires in the kitchen result in major property damage and often claim at least one or two lives. In our case, all we had lost was a pressure cooker and a kitchen mat -- a far better result than we could have expected! By this point, I did start to shake a little and all I could think of was the two girls that had died when I was a young boy.

***

The power of intention is undeniable. When our purpose and determination are strong enough, pure enough and clear enough, we can achieve anything, even when the odds are stacked against us. As long as we focus on our intention, strengthen it and eliminate anything that might weaken it, we can achieve our goals.

Allah Subhana wa ta'ala is Al-Qadir and Al-Hakeem, the All-Capable and All-Wise, and He gives us many signs in His creation. Making intention is just like sowing seeds. Imagine, for example, if when planting a seed, you had to take responsibility for bringing life from the inorganic world to the organic world to actually make the plant grow. Imagine if you had to operate the photosynthetic process every day and you had to physically create the plant stems and cells and enrich them with colour. Making just one plant would be hard enough but making thousands of thousands every year would be impossible! Even scientists have yet to discover how to create a plant that can work in the same way that Allah Subhana wa ta'ala has perfectly created and provided for us. Such is the perfection of Allah's power and wisdom.

But Alhumdulillah, Allah is merciful and doesn't burden us with this responsibility. All we have to do is plant the seed, water it and protect it from pests and predators. And just like with sowing seeds, we have only to make our intention sincere and strong, keep renewing it and nurturing it and prevent doubts from weakening or killing it. Our job, after making our intention, is to put forth our most sincere and best effort; Allah is the one who will bring to fruition the result of our efforts (pun intended) according to His infinite wisdom. The human mind is limited, and often we cannot perceive with our rational minds how something can be done, but Allah's wisdom and knowledge is infinite, and as we dispose our affairs to Him, He Subhana wa ta'ala opens for us the way.

There are many plants that are known to grow even in the harshest of climates. Allah makes the way for them to grow. So make your intentions, put forth your efforts and dispose your affairs to Him.

14 CHAPTER

GRAVITY:
LIVING BY THE PHYSICAL AND SPIRITUAL LAWS

" Whoever makes the dunya his most important matter, Allah will confound his affairs and make poverty appear before his eyes and he will not get anything from the world except what has been decreed for him. Whoever makes the akhirah his most important matter, Allah will settle his affairs and make him content in his heart and the dunya will come to him although he does not want it".

Prophet Muhammad (peace be upon him)

As Wasiq moved into a new home, he decided to park his car in the driveway which was a sunken drive below the level of the road, with the neighbour's drive adjacent. The neighbour had new block paving installed and had added a rigid wall less than ten inches high to signal the end of the paving as a boundary and to protect their drive. As Wasiq drove his car in, he misjudged the edge of the driveway, and his front-left tyre rolled slightly onto the neighbour's paving boundary. He re-adjusted his steering to correct his misjudgement; as he did so, the car slipped off the boundary wall and caught him by surprise. Thankfully there was no major damage, but he realised it had not been a smart thing to do. But now that it was done he got out and inspected the tyre. Sure enough there was evidence of potential damage to the tyre wall. Since it was the end of the working day, he decided there was nothing he could do at the moment and that he'd see to the matter in the morning. Most likely he would have to replace the tyre.

In the morning, he inspected the tyre once again, and to his surprise, it wasn't flat as he had expected it to be, but in reality, it still had plenty of air in it. He decided to drive down to the nearest tyre dealer. He pulled up in their parking lot and explained to the sales rep what had happened. The rep inspected the tyre and told Wasiq that the damage to the tyre was purely superficial and that the tyre wall was intact making it perfectly safe to continue driving. He asked if there was a charge for the inspection, since he wasn't buying a new tyre, to which the rep replied 'not necessary'.

Relieved, he drove home and as he pulled up to the house, he noticed his elder brother had decided to park his car in the driveway instead. Wasiq himself parked on the street and as he walked in, he noticed his brother had made the same mistake with the boundary wall that he'd made the night before. Only this time the damage seemed more severe. The tyre was completely punctured and disfigured, and the wheel itself looked like it had seen better days. His brother was on the phone to the car recovery services who had dispatched a recovery vehicle to the house. The recovery agent arrived, inspected the damage and said the car needed to be taken to a repair centre, since not only had the tyre been damaged but also the brake system, the ABS and the wheel. After two days in the workshop, the car was delivered back home along with a bill in excess of $2000.

Clearly the first brother got "lucky". Or did he?

Imagine an adult that didn't know what gravity was: this grown person never realised that gravity is a force of nature with laws to be recognised and effects to be observed. Life for such an adult would be a disaster.

This person would, for example, walk out on a ledge and fall and then suffer from serious injury and pain. But worse still, instead of admitting responsibility for his accident and blaming himself for his ignorance regarding gravity, he would blame "bad luck" or lament whatever he had done to receive this "punishment" from Allah Subhana wa ta'ala.

It is an extreme and far-fetched example, I know, but the point is that just as there are undeniable and unchangeable physical laws in nature, there also exist undeniable and unchangeable laws in the spiritual world (i.e. the realm of the unseen, al-ghaib). As with those who learn to recognise and respect the physical laws and their own relative limitations, those who recognise and respect the laws of the unseen and understand their relative limitations learn how to navigate life achieving much of what they want and avoiding what they don't.

In the story above, Wasiq always strove to make sure that his income was halal. While his older brother's income was not. Wasiq had chosen a halal income because he understood the barakah it places in one's wealth and purchases. His brother clearly didn't recognise this unseen law, and he suffered the consequences. These are the kind of things science doesn't give answers for.

The laws of the unseen are those laws that Islam guides us to, the rules that Allah Subhana wa ta'ala has set forth for mankind to follow. And just like there are consequences and results for disregarding or following the physical laws (i.e. ignoring gravity and falling off a ledge or respecting gravity and remaining on firm ground), so, too, are there consequences and results for disregarding or following the laws of the unseen (i.e. the laws of Allah). With both types of laws, the physical and the unseen, effects may be immediate or delayed. For example, gravity - is a physical law, and the effects gravity can be seen immediately, but the laws that govern climate change have effects that are much slower to appear. On the other hand, the effects of following or disregarding laws of spirituality may not be as easily identified to the observer (unless he has acquired the knowledge about the ways of Allah from the Qur'an and hadith), but we know they exist. For example, when a child is conceived out of wedlock, we know that in the practical world this has some impact, but in the spiritual world it has severe consequences. These are the unseen laws.

Allah constantly reminds us in the Qur'an that He is the Lord of the unseen and that believers "believe in the unseen". From the viewpoint of the believer, respecting and obeying the laws of the unseen is of the utmost importance.

***

I had been working on a digital marketing contract, and the nature of the contract was such that I was paid by the hour. I was working from home one day and signed in onto the project management system. I was leading the project for the marketing department, and the staff had a habit of disappearing right at the moment we were supposed to meet or discuss plans for the project. One Tuesday morning, the usual happened. I signed in, and as I awaited a reply to a question in the project management system, I got a text message from the marketing coordinator to say that he had been pulled away and would be with me in 15 mins or so. Past experience told me that it was going to be more than the stated 15 mins. There were other matters related to the project that I could have been getting on with while I waited, but I reasoned with myself that if he wasn't prepared to prioritise this project, then neither was I.

So, I decided to do my laundry instead. As I put the whites into the washing machine, the cleaner asked me if she should throw away all the fruit and vegetables in the bottom shelf of the fridge as it was no longer fit for eating. I explained to her that it couldn't be possible since I'd only just bought the groceries the night before. She pointed to the fridge's temperature setting and explained to me that I had set the temperature too low and it had caused the fresh fruit to spoil. Annoyed with myself, I finished off the whites as she did away with the spoilt fruit. As I walked back into the kitchen, I decided to take my Vitamin D supplement. As I reached for the bottle to take it out of the cupboard, my hand caught another powdered supplement, clipped it and caused it to fall on the kitchen counter, breaking the lid and pouring about a third of its contents on the floor. If I wasn't annoyed already, I was definitely annoyed now. I started wondering what I had done to deserve this 'punishment' from Allah.

Then I did something rather unusual for me; I decided to tally up the cost of the damage I had caused myself that morning and quantify it in terms of the number of hours I would have to work on the digital marketing contract to earn that back. I counted the cost of the thrown fruit and vegetables and the amount of wasted supplement and then compared it to how much I was paid per hour by my client. I discovered that it would take me 26 minutes to replace the cost of what had been thrown away. By this time the marketing co-ordinator had returned to his desk, and we were able to resume. I was pretty sure it had been more than 15 minutes as he'd promised, so I checked the time between his first text message to me and his return. Amazingly, it was exactly 26 minutes! SubhanAllah, my act of cheating my client out of 26 minutes of work, resulted in a direct loss of 26 mins to me personally! Surely, Allah is Al-Adl, the Most Just!

It's important to honour our contracts to have barakah in our wealth. In this case, my contract was geared such that I was charging for my time, so I should have either charged less for when I wasn't available, or I should have gotten on with other things in the project.

Honesty and fairness are just two of the laws of the unseen that the Prophetic model teaches us. There are many more like this. (And yes, I've long since learned my lesson). The point is that the sooner we make ourselves aware of these laws, the sooner we can stop lamenting our fate for outcomes we don't desire.

***

Unfortunately, in our modern day, we spend most of our lives dreaming of being financially free. We marry later and start our families later and later all because we've tied ourselves down to financial slavery.

Our faulty understanding of money as an agent of corruption for the morally corrupt often prevents us from taking action to build wealth. Many of us are still handicapped by the idea that to build wealth is something that is only the preserve of the hedonistic, greedy or lustful. An idea often perpetuated by the media.

Just like the media often perpetuates the idea that most deaths in the West are from acts of terrorism, or that most Muslims are terrorists, even though actual data proves otherwise, in the same vein the media often perpetuates the idea that being wealthy is only for those that get lucky or build wealth through unethical means.

The media, through its incessant need to sell papers via sensationalism, either flaunts the successful entrepreneur as an unrivalled genius, a product of divine luck, or with a questionable history.

As I write this, Manoj Bhargava – a billionaire - is spending over 99% of his wealth trying to change the lives of poor people in Africa through giving them self-sustaining systems for access to clean water, better healthcare and energy. A man of simple tastes and simple living, whose name is nowhere to be seen in the general mainstream media. It's only because he is taking his narrative into his own hands that some of us have learned of him.

Instead, the mainstream press chooses to focus on the billionaire that leads a hedonistic lifestyle indulging in cruises, yachts, women and drugs, or the Saudi Oil Tycoon who owns a mansion with 100 bedrooms, 25 wives and a car constructed out of pure silver made on special order by Audi. Occasionally we get to hear about the white man that plans to take man to Mars. But there is no mention of a man from humble beginnings say from Lucknow, India, until a day his works become so well-known that the press has no choice but to write about him so they can market to and appease his ever growing base of supporters.

How many times have you heard or thought – "Money corrupts"?

It's due to the mainstream media ideas of what a billionaire is that we remain in a perpetual state of inaction. The idea seems so inaccessible that we don't even bother to consider it possible, let alone give it a try. Yet money is only an amplifier. It can only magnify the kind of person we already are. If we're kind and generous human beings, then more money will only give us more resources to become more kind and more generous. But if more money makes us more malicious or narcissistic, then those traits were already present in the first place. They didn't suddenly appear because of money.

It's like giving someone a powerful car. One person might use it to screech tyres on the road, blast loud music, drive dangerously, cause mayhem on the street and put people's lives in danger. Another person might use the same car to do a charity run, make an impression on clients, travel long distances to meet relatives, take the family on a nice holiday and make the lives of family and neighbours better in any way possible. The person's character and values that led to the way he chose to make use of the car didn't come in the car's glove compartment. Those qualities were already there, in that individual's nature; the car was merely a tool to further express or act according to theses innate traits.

No one ever asks themselves if a car is going to corrupt them, so why should we be suspicious that money will do so?

Whatever character faults we exhibit should cause us to blame ourselves, not money and definitely not Allah. We're all too busy telling ourselves that if we had a lot of money, that Allah might punish us, He might be unhappy with us. But would Allah punish us for possessing a sandwich? What about 100 sandwiches? What about 1000 sandwiches? Or 100,000 sandwiches? Surely, we'd be so grateful that Allah gave us the opportunity to do something good with all those sandwiches. We wouldn't keep them all for ourselves, perhaps enough for us and our loved ones, but the rest we would give to others.

It is not having money that corrupts, but rather it is the position that the person gives to money that will either make him subservient to wealth or will make his wealth work for him. Ibn Qayyim al-Jawziyyah was very astute in his observation about money and corruption when he said: "When there is money in your hand and not in your heart, it will not harm you even if it is a lot; and when it is in your heart, it will harm you even if there is none in your hands"

Many people don't know that of the ten sahaba who were promised paradise Uthman ibn Affan and Abdur-Rahman ibn 'Awf (may Allah be pleased with them) were very wealthy. (However, even though they are known as having been blessed by Allah with material wealth, both of these men experienced extremely difficult financial times in their lives as well, especially in the early days in Medina). Great wealth is not looked down upon or discouraged in Islam, but the focus is on what a person does with it. Indeed, the legacies of Uthman ibn Affan and Abdur-Rahman ibn 'Awf are not merely legacies of wealth; they are legacies of taqwa, (the fear of Allah) and great generosity.

Uthman (may Allah be pleased with him) was a wise businessman. Once during a time of drought in Medina, there was a well owned by a Jew who would charge the Muslims very high amounts to fill their buckets with water. They complained to the Prophet (peace be upon him) who said that whoever bought that well would be promised Jannah. Uthman went to the Jew and offered to buy the well. After some bargaining, he finally agreed to sell Uthman 1/2 of the well for an excessive amount of money. Uthman made the deal; the Jew would have the right to sell the water one day, and Uthman would have the rights to the water the next.

Uthman (may Allah be pleased with him) went to the Muslims and told them to take water for free on his day and that they should take enough to cover their needs for two days. And that is what they did. On the day of Uthman's right, the Muslims would take water without charge, and on the day of the Jew's right, no one would come for water. In the end, the Jew realized he would not be able to make any more money off of the well, so he sold the remaining 1/2 to Uthman (peace be upon him). Uthman in turn made the well a waqf or endowment for the Muslims. Until today, the well and the land around it and all of its produce and all of its subsequent profits belong to the coffer of the Muslims. The well of Uthman is a true example of sadiqah jariyah!

And what about Abdur-Rahman ibn 'Awf? There is a well-known story about AbdurRahman from the time after the Prophet (peace be upon him) had died. One day in Medina there was a great rising of sand and tremoring of the ground. When A'ishah (may Allah be pleased with her) heard this, she asked what was happening in Medina. She was told that it was just the caravan of AbdurRahman ibn Awf returning to Medina with 700 camels. Upon hearing this A'ishah mentioned that she remembered the Prophet (peace be upon him) saying that he had seen Abdur-Rahman Ibn 'Awf "crawling into Paradise'.

What did Abdur-Rahman ibn 'Awf do when these words reached him? He immediately went to the house of A'ishah and told her to bear witness that the caravan and all it carried were being given as sadaqah, charity for the sake of Allah Subhana wa ta'ala. The loads of the 700 camels were all distributed amongst the people in Medina and the surrounding areas.

If you're a kind and generous person that earns $1000 each month and gives 10% of your money to charity every month, then there's a very good chance that if you were earning $100,000 a month, you'd still give 10% of your income to charity. But if a person can't bring himself to give even $5 in charity despite having $50 in the bank, then who's to say he would give $500,000 when he has $5 million in the bank?

Whatever is holding us back from acquiring wealth is not money, intelligence, luck or skill set. Nor is it what little we have to start with, but rather it is how we feel about money. Our relationship with money is what governs our ability to earn more, and for the majority of Muslims, this relationship is in dire straits.

There are many things that affect our relationship with money, a large part of which comes from our parents, who in turn developed their own relationship with money that they learned from their parents, and so on and so on.

T. Harv Eker writes in Secrets of the Millionare Mind:

"You've probably heard the saying "Monkey see, monkey do.""

Well, humans aren't far behind. As kids, we learn just about everything from modeling. Although most of us would hate to admit it, there's more than a grain of truth in the old saying "The apple doesn't fall too far from the tree." This reminds me of the story about a woman who prepares a ham for dinner by cutting off both ends. Her bewildered husband asks why she cuts off the ends. She replies, "That's how my mom cooked it." Well, it just so happened that her mom was coming for dinner that night. So they asked her why she cut off the ends of the ham. Mom replies, "That's how my mom cooked it." So they decide to call Grandma on the phone and ask why she cut off the ends of the ham. Her answer? "Because my pan was too small!" The point is that generally speaking, we tend to be identical to one or a combination of our parents in the arena of money."

So, we've formed these ideas and behaviors from our parents, who picked it up from theirs, and somewhere along the line, somewhere in that chain, somebody's gotten the idea that having money is not a good thing. Then these adopted assumptions are reinforced by the media.

***

Whether we choose to admit it or not, most of us believe that money is the root of all evil. Even if we don't openly acknowledge this belief, our actions always betray us because action comes from thought which is belief manifest. No one jumps on a prayer mat at dhuhr time if they don't believe that they should be worshipping Allah and seeking His reward. Therefore, if someone believes that money is the root of all evil he or she would go to great lengths to avoid acquiring it.

It is pseudo-Christian concepts such as this that need to change. Money is not the root of all evil. It's nothing but a means to achieve our higher goals.

Although Islam does prohibit us from hoarding wealth, there is nothing in Islam to discourage us from attaining it. In fact, the following hadith indicates quite the opposite. Abu Hurayrah (may Allah be pleased with him) narrated that the Messenger of Allah (peace be upon him) said:

"The upper hand is better than the lower hand (i.e., the spending hand is better than the receiving hand); and begin (charity) with those who are under your care; and the best charity is that which given out of surplus; and he who asks (Allah) to help him abstain from the unlawful and the forbidden, Allah will fulfill his wish; and he who seeks self-sufficiency will be made self-sufficient by Allah." (Sahih Bukhari)

This hadith is evidence that it is more desirable for the believer to be not only self-sufficient, having enough to provide for himself and his family, but to have wealth above and beyond his needs that can be given in charity.

Wealth is a great means to create for ourselves financial freedom. It is financial freedom that releases us from the immobilizing obligation to go to work every day, that enables us to work on what our hearts really desire and that frees us to worship Allah in the best ways possible and to work on our higher purpose NOW. The shackles of financial slavery, on the other hand, intimidate us into procrastination and self-deceiving plans to pursue these goals when we are older and have reached the age of retirement -- even though none of us is promised to live that long!

We need to move away from the myth that wealth can only be attained through exceptionally hard work. Yes, entrepreneurial and financial success take hard work, but it's no harder than the work we do in our full time jobs. I personally know many people that earn well and have reached entrepreneurial success by working less hard than they would in a full time job. That's not to say they didn't work hard, but it is to say they didn't work any harder than they would have done in a full time job. The effort is the same, so why not apply it to something that will have more meaning in our lives?

Many people feel that having a large amount of money is a large responsibility, but it's not as if there are huge wads of cash we need to store under the bed, or a million money-balls we need to take care of in a ball putt, it's just more digits in our bank account. You probably have millions of lines of codes sitting in some file on your computer right now. Does it feel like a huge burden and responsibility?

Whatever the beliefs, thoughts and ideas you have about money right now, most are likely to be false and should be re-evaluated.

But probably the greatest limiting belief we all possess regarding money is that of our understanding of abundance and worthiness.

If we go back to the analogy of the sandwich, nobody ever asks themselves if they want to make a sandwich or if they are actually worthy of having a sandwich.

In fact, put everything that you think is true about money into a sentence; now, try saying that sentence replacing the word 'money' with the word 'sandwich'. 'Sandwiches' are the root of all evil. Only people that have 'sandwiches' can make more 'sandwiches'. People with 'sandwiches' get more 'sandwiches', and people with less 'sandwiches' get less and less. If I suddenly had a lot of 'sandwiches', I'd mutate into a very greedy and corrupted miser. I can't make myself a 'sandwich' because there isn't enough bread to go around. I'm not smart enough to learn how to make a 'sandwich'.

And my favourite one: I don't feel like I deserve a 'sandwich'. Making 'sandwiches' is really hard. You have to work long hours, sacrifice family and friends for many years before you learn how to make a 'sandwich'. Allah chose to bless certain people with 'sandwiches' but not me; I must have sinned and therefore He is punishing me, by not letting me figure out how to make a 'sandwich'.

The bottom line is that people don't feel worthy of money, they don't feel that they deserve money, they don't feel that they're good enough or they feel that they're being punished with poverty. But let me ask you this question: if you don't have a sandwich right now, do you say to yourself you don't have a sandwich because Allah is punishing you or is it because you don't have a sandwich because a) you didn't make the decision that you wanted a sandwich and b) even if you did make the decision that you wanted a sandwich you didn't get off the sofa and actually go make it.

See how ludicrous this all sounds?

The fundamental truth is this: you never made the decision to just go for it. Instead, you're blaming your qadr and blaming Allah for punishing you, whereas in fact, we have been ordered to have the very best thought and expectations of Allah, and when we do, we will find that not only does He fulfill our expectations, but He Subhana wa ta'ala exceeds them by His Infinite Mercy and Graciousness.

The Prophet (peace be upon him) said: Allah the Most High said, 'I am as My servant thinks (expects) I am. I am with him when he mentions Me. If he mentions Me to himself, I mention him to Myself; and if he mentions Me in an assembly, I mention him in an assembly greater than it. If he draws near to Me a hand's length, I draw near to him an arm's length. And if he comes to Me walking, I go to him at speed.'" (Sahih Bukhari).

Sadly, by choosing to believe Allah has decreed us to be deprived of wealth or is punishing us by keeping us poor, we do ourselves a disservice by succumbing to fatalism and having a poor opinion of Him. We should turn our lenses inward and question whether we ever chose to make the decision and exert the effort to attain wealth in the first place.

Ibn al-Qayyim (may Allah have Mercy upon him) said:

Most people – in fact, all of them except those protected by Allah – assume other than the truth, and assume the worst. Most people believe that they are deprived of their rights, have bad luck, deserve more than what Allah gave them, and it is as if they are saying: 'My Lord has wronged me and deprived me of what I deserve,' and his soul bears witness to this while his tongue denies it and refuses to openly state this. And whoever digs into his soul and comes to know its ins and outs will see this in it like fire in a triggered explosion...And if you dig into anyone's soul, you will see that he blames fate and would rather have something else happen to him than what actually did, and that things should be this way or that...So, dig into your own self: are you protected from this? If you are safe from this, you have been protected from something great. Otherwise, I do not see that you have been saved. [Zad al-Ma'ad]

Another myth people too readily believe is that you can only make money if you're really intelligent. Well, do you have to be really intelligent to make a sandwich? No. Do you have to be lucky? Are you only going to make it in business if you get lucky? Again, replace it with a sandwich; do you have to get lucky to make a sandwich? No, you make the decision that you want to eat a sandwich, and you go and eat it. It's no different than money; money is still just another object. There's no special rule that applies to money that applies to everything else. Money is given way more import (in this context) than it actually deserves.

Money has been made into this unachievable thing because we hear stories about "heroes" and about how hard they worked to get their big break. Some of us have been conditioned to erroneously believe that the poor man is more pious. In fact, many of us even romanticize the idea of poverty. That is the worst. Remember, "the upper hand is better than the lower hand", and the impoverished are, characteristically speaking, "the lower hand".

Then there's the other myth that you can only make money if you have money to start.

The truth is, however, that if you can't turn $5 into $10 then you're certainly not going to be able to turn $5 million into $10 million. Just look at Donald Trump. Studies suggest, when adjusted for inflation, that if Donald Trump hadn't invested any of his money since the early 70s, he'd be richer than he is now. Donald Trump has consistently lost money over his career. It's true he started off with more money than the rest of us, but he's actually not that great at making money. The only real advantage people have that start with money is that they have the potential to make money faster. It's just simple math. The larger sum of money you start with, the more money you have as a net sum when you double it. But the limiting factor isn't what you start with, it's how much you can multiply it.

If someone has the capability and muscle to fill up a gas tank with 10 liters of fuel, the skill doesn't change to load it with 100 liters of fuel or 1,000 liters of fuel. It's just a difference in quantity. So, for someone to say who's already filled a 50 liter gas tank to say he can't fill a tank with 1000 liters of fuel is like him saying he suddenly doesn't know how to pump the gas because the tank is bigger. Why should anything change just because he needs more fuel now? The muscle used to get more gas doesn't change. All he has to do is hold the fuel nozzle longer until it reaches 1000 liters. There's no difference in the skill or intelligence or luck or anything like that, that is required, but yet, just because the number (fuel requirement) got bigger. Suddenly, the excuse comes out, "Can't do it" even though just minutes prior, the skill was there to pump the gas and fill the tank.

Doesn't that sound a little…. well…ludicrous?

To be fair, many people have negative multipliers, even seemingly wealthy people such as Donald Trump; many high profile footballers, actors and other celebrities end up declaring bankruptcy when their career takes a slight dip because they never learned to grow their money in the first place. They only learned to apply a negative multiplier (I.e. spending it) instead of multiplying it (i.e making the money work hard for them).

It's like saying, "Well, there are all these other people that have all these sandwiches. They are so blessed by God. They are so amazing. There is something about them that is so great. But, I'M not capable of having a sandwich". There's a sandwich store right next to you, where you can walk in and actually order a sandwich but you keep telling yourself, "I can't do it. I'm not capable of doing it", and if you're telling yourself that, then you will create your own truth. It's never going to come to you; you will never have that sandwich!

So, if you think to yourself, money is really hard to make or is only reserved for those that start off with a silver spoon then ask yourself, is a sandwich really hard to make? If the answer to making a sandwich is really easy then making money is really easy as well. If you say to yourself, "Yeah, but I want to buy something but I don't have any money right now." Then ask yourself what would you do, if you didn't have any bread right now to make a sandwich, you just go and get some more bread. There's enough bread in the world, there's

105

enough money in the world.

Whatever you believe about money just replace that with a sandwich and then ask yourself, does it make sense with a sandwich? And if it doesn't make sense with a sandwich, it doesn't make sense with money.

15 CHAPTER

THE MOST OVERLOOKED DAWAH OPPORTUNITY OF OUR TIME: SUNNAH AS A BEST BUSINESS PRACTICE

"Start a business of worshipping Allah, and all types of profits will come to you without needing any capital."

Malik ibn Dinar

One day, as I walked into my prospective client's office, I wondered to myself if my client (whom I will respectfully refer to as Uncle) would remember our appointment.

Uncle owns an Asian takeaway-cum-restaurant situated in the town centre of a popular Muslim neighbourhood. He and I had met several times during the regular meetings held at a non-profit which was involved in helping the masjid and local community. Uncle would often provide the food at the meetings from his restaurant -- completely free of charge, without any expectation for favour in return. Though Uncle knew of me, he didn't know me personally.

So when I discovered that he was looking for help with the next phase of growth for his business, I decided to call him and organise a time to pay him a visit. I promised him I'd take a look at his business and see what I could do to help. I ended my phone call by asking him to put the date and time of the meeting in his diary.

On my way from the car park to his office and as I tried to determine the actual office location, I maneuvered past overflowing rubbish bins, inconveniently parked cars and water filled potholes. Based on my prior experiences, such signs indicated that he had most probably forgotten our meeting and was unlikely to be waiting for me.

Having worked with many Muslim businesses, I fully expected him to either have completely forgotten about the meeting (having not diarised it) or to offer some 'legitimate excuse' as to why today's meeting needed to be re-scheduled for another time. I've gotten used to having my time wasted. If there's one thing many of us can agree on, it is that, some cultures don't value the sanctity of someone else's time the way they should.

Alhamdulillah I was pleasantly surprised to find Uncle ready and waiting for me. Uncle was dressed in a black shalwar kameez, with a formal blazer on top. Unusual business attire, but for him it seemed to work. As I sat down to begin discussing Uncle's business, I congratulated him on the success of his take-away franchise thus far.

Uncle has been running this franchise business for the last 12 years and, alhamdullilah, has experienced consistent business growth, year after year.

Though I am very well-versed with what it takes to grow a business (after all, that is why clients hire me), I was keen to learn what 'magic ingredient' had been driving the growth of his business thus far.

As we started to discuss the plans for business growth, Uncle took me through some of the plans he and his business partner had already been working on. I then prodded further to get a better understanding of the business. I was interested to learn about the kind of staff he employed and the training methods he used. Uncle told me that when he first started his business, each new employee was trained to treat each customer not as a customer, but as a guest. He told me that the reason this policy was implemented was because of the importance Islam places on the treatment of one's guests

It seemed I had discovered the 'magic ingredient' to the success of his business: Uncle was practically applying the sunnah of the Prophet Muhammad (peace be upon him), and the result was an undeniable manifestation of barakah in the business. He then went on to tell me that each employee was told not to short-change customers. If the customer ordered five chicken wings, then they were to receive five chicken wings. The training regimen even went as far as suggesting that if by mistake the customer received six chicken wings, it was better that the restaurant lose money than lose barakah by short-changing the customer. After all, every employee had to answer to Allah for their actions, and as the owner, Uncle said that he didn't want to be held responsible not dealing fairly with his customers on the Day of Judgement. Subhanallah! What an amazing ethos!

This kind of beautiful conduct reminded me of a previous client from earlier that year. When my consulting engagement with this client had finished, I sent him an invoice for the remainder of payment. My client, a Muslim brother who owned a minicab firm, called me and presented me with three options for receiving payment.

He said: "I can send you a bank transfer, but the payment will probably reach you tomorrow morning since we're nearing the close of the day, or I have cash waiting on my table, you're free to come and collect it today, or if you would prefer the money even sooner, then I can arrange for a taxi driver to bring the cash to you within the hour".

I was reminded of the hadith of the Prophet (peace be upon him) when he said: "Give the worker his wages before his sweat dries" (Sunan Ibn Majah). This brother had clearly taken the words of the

Prophet (peace be upon him) to heart and acted upon them. I was so incredibly touched by this brother's commitment to pay me on time and even quicker than my expectations. Imagine if such conduct was making me, another Muslim, feel this way, then what would the effects be on non-Muslims if they experienced such treatment from Muslim business owners?

Then there is the story of the lady who was looking to buy a Nutri Bullet juicer because her mum had cancer. When Cara Grace Duggan tried to buy the juicer from a classified listings sale, the gentleman selling the juicer learned of her mum's condition so offered to send the Nutri Bullet to her free of charge. She thanked him for the kind offer but politely refused out of courtesy; she then received a follow-up text message that confirmed the dispatch of a brand new Nutri-Bullet.

The "kind man" placed the order for a brand new Nutri-Bullet to arrive to Cara's mum as soon as possible as he didn't want her mum to have to wait. Cara Grace was so touched by the "huge act" of kindness, that she shared the story on Facebook. Her post went viral until it was finally covered in a national newspaper. There are no details about who the man was, but I wouldn't be surprised if he were a Muslim, not just because the transcript of the text messages made it obvious that English wasn't his first language (increasing the likelihood that he was a Muslim emigrant), but the reality is that, generally speaking. Muslims have a greater capacity and inclination to be so gracious and exhibit such beautiful conduct. After all we're taught by the best example sent to mankind (peace be upon him).

If one random act of kindness can have such a profound effect on so many people, then imagine, what multiple, purposeful acts of kindness by Muslims in different parts of the world can have on nations as a whole.

The point is that there are so many Muslim businesses interacting on a daily basis with non-Muslims. Every single day, there are hundreds of thousands of opportunities, if not millions of opportunities, around the globe for us, as Muslims, to show others what beauty of character really is. Better yet, the additional effect of which -- especially in today's world of increased competition and market

110

saturation -- is that not only does it put barakah into our businesses but it also serves to grow them. In a world where the consumer has more and more choice, companies can no longer rely on mass distribution alone. Customers want better and better customer experiences.

Now is our chance to differentiate ourselves from other businesses by providing better customer experiences. We have at our disposal the best training manual on gracious conduct in the detailed accounts of the interactions of our beloved Prophet (peace be upon him). His legacy, his Sunnah, his teachings and guidance have been captured and preserved for us in the narrations of his hadith. Isn't it time for us to put his legacy into practice? We are guaranteed to reap the benefits of our efforts not only in our business here in dunya but also in what we will be given in akhirah. So what are we waiting for?

By making a serious commitment to beautify the character of our businesses, we can show non-Muslims the real beauty of our religion. A'ishah (may Allah be pleased with her) narrated that the Prophet (peace be upon him) said: "Kindness is not to be found in anything, but that it adds to its beauty; and it is not withdrawn from anything but it makes it defective" (Sahih Muslim).

If every Muslim business owner were to make a serious commitment to put these words into practice, then in a relatively short time, non-Muslims would learn to associate Muslims with the most honorable qualities and interactions, instead of the 'ugly' narratives that are pushed to the forefront every day. We would be doing a great service to the spreading of Islam and increasing the weight of good deeds in our scales.

When the sahabah "opened" up a new city there were two things that they always did first; one they built a masjid, and two, they established a market.

As Muslims, we've emigrated to all corners of the earth and built masajid wherever we have landed, but we haven't built the platforms that enable trade, commerce and interaction. We have neglected the vital opportunities to take our own trade to the rest of the world and to demonstrate that we have the integrity and character to be leaders of

111

the world, both in spirituality and in commerce.

This is an incredibly overlooked opportunity since modern systems of trade and commerce have the potential to spread incredibly fast. The time for a new platform to reach critical mass gets smaller and smaller every decade. Where television took more than two decades to reach critical mass, Facebook took only half a decade. Snapchat took just a few months.

Facebook started out as a simple website for college students to interact, and now it's a global phenomenon with over one billion users who share their personal lives with each other every single day. This is a good example of a modern structure that enables trade, commerce and interaction.

Again, it's a modern structure that is not restricted to being the mainstay or sole preserve of tech companies.

Henry Ford wanted to "belt" the entire earth with cars. His vision made him determined to export his idea to the rest of the world. He, along with taking cars to the rest of the world, also exported his ideas of capitalism. Now, not a single country in the world lacks possession of a motor vehicle industry in one form or another, along with the same capitalistic ideas of employment, wages and labour.

It's appropriate to remember the role of Islamic merchants who travelled to different lands such as Indonesia. Taking a look at the crucial part they played in its historical context helps us understand why Indonesia has the largest Muslim population in the world. These merchants weren't just coming to do business. Trade was the vehicle for exporting ideas, and the impressive character of these Muslim merchants was fundamental in the spreading of the teachings of Islam, of the belief in the oneness of Allah, of the importance of good character and of the necessity to establish peace and justice.

These merchants exhibited such exemplary character that the people they encountered were intrigued. They were impressed by the Muslim merchants because they didn't cheat on price and weren't driven by greed. The Muslim merchants honoured their contracts and were incredibly generous. They showed far less concern and worry about their wealth and the need to earn a living because they knew that all provision, all rizq was from Allah. They treated those that worked with them as peers, as comrades, rather than as slaves.

These wonderous qualities caused the people they met to reflect on the manners of the men they had met and to question their own practises. They wondered if these honest merchants could have such exemplary conduct in trade, a conduct which was dictated by their religion, then what else must their religion be teaching them about life in general? Good conduct and honest trading opened minds, and made strangers see that this religion was far more holistic than other religions and that it wasn't restricted to ritualistic worship.

If we are to take the beauty of Islam to the rest of the world, we must recognise that trade is an indispensable vehicle for doing so. We must also recognise that the quality of our trade is directly proportional to the impact we have on society. We must remember that no matter what personal gain we might acquire through our entrepreneurship, it is our positive contributions to society and our commitment to making the world a better place that have the greatest value in the end.

The better we trade, the better we impact society.

16 CHAPTER

THE AGE OF WISDOM:
POWER PLAYS FROM PAST TO FUTURE

"Crises [with a capital-C] ... function like laboratories in which the future is incubated. They have given us agriculture and the industrial revolution, technology and the labour contract, killer germs and antibiotics. Once they strike, the past ceases to be a reliable predictor of the future and a brave new world is born."

Yanis Varoufakis

In the beginning, in the Age of Man, those that won were those that had might, physical strength. People with might and great force had power in society; they attained a higher status. The leader was the cave man that could run faster, had more strength, could hunt better and force his will over others. He caught the most meat and the weak turned to him and depended on him.

Then there was the Age of Labour. In this age, those that had more man-power dominated society. They would wield power in society through sheer number of men. These were the Pharaohs, the Romans, the Persians and others with gigantic armies.

But then came the Age of Industry. In this time, it wasn't about strength or man-power any more. It wasn't about labour but about industry. Those that had better equipment and better processes won in society through the power of leveraging information. An example of this is when Napoleon entered the Muslim lands and spread information rapidly via the printing press. This ability to spread his own version of "knowledge" better and faster than the rest gave him and his allies the upper hand, and thus began the start of the colossal western empires. Over time, as they developed their industry, those who knew where to find the world's resources, such as oil and gold, and how best to extract them were the people that could shape society to their will.

Now we're in the Information Age, where knowledge itself is no longer power. Google brought Information to our fingertips. Now those who wield power in society are those that have wisdom. They know what best to do with the knowledge they acquire. It's not the man that has all the facts, but he who knows what to do with them. It's like two men looking at an x-ray of a broken bone; both can see the bone is broken, but only the one who has the wisdom of what to do with that knowledge can remedy the situation.

I personally believe that given how fast technology is moving -- with major headway being made in areas of artificial intelligence, big data and an ever-increasing array of connected devices – the next age to arrive will be the Age of Wisdom. In the Age of Wisdom, those that establish the best morality will be the ones that yield power over society. Businesses built around morality will be ones that will lead in society. Men that win will be the ones that have the best moral grounding and understanding. We've already seen some examples of this, through how quickly movements have grown when they've chosen to democratize power to replace tyranny or bureaucracy. Take Uber, AirBnB, Twitter, eBay as just a handful of examples of many. Granted, in many cases, many movements have replaced the existing tyranny with new muscle-flexings of their own. Uber, for example, circumvented the decades-old tyranny of the Taxi medallions, but then used its power to implement things like surge pricing, and Facebook is well known for applying a double-standard of censoring some types of content and not others.

This can be seen in most of the West now. Good ethical commerce only equates to wider justice when it is absolute.

Everywhere we turn, thought leaders are talking about democratizing this and democratizing that. We see companies win that provide the best customer experiences, that commit themselves not just to revenue or profit but to customer success. Simple changes in economic and operating models are not to be under-estimated. It's these inherent ethics that businesses choose to adopt that predispose them to such rapid rise. This turn in emphasis can lead to dramatic shifts in power in a very short space of time.

But there will be a split.

Those who know understand that the entities controlling the balance of power will vie to centralise their power by either manipulating or liberating the people (faux pas ethics or superficial veneers of morality). Those who manipulate are likely to win first until people demand liberation which will come when they see the illusion being fed to them; then they will seek truth through justice and morality.

Given how society has evolved through the ages so far, and taking into account what Islam teaches of the signs before the Day of Judgment, I believe that if we're to lead in society, we cannot relegate ourselves to the pursuit of just knowledge and wisdom. We inherently have to build models -- be they business models, economic models, operating models, modes of delivery or experience – upon solid moral frameworks.

Now it's a game of ethics.

He who has the best ethics wins…eventually.

Afterword

The Muslim entrepreneur is in a prime position to impact and change the world – and to change it for the better. With Islam guiding his intentions and manners, the Muslim will be motivated by the highest and most noble of causes – pleasing his Creator and working towards Jannah. The Muslim is equipped for success when he or she internalizes the two-faceted reality: the Hereafter is everlasting with Jannah being the ultimate win, and dunya is temporary and full of distraction and deception. This perspective allows the Muslim entrepreneur to apply acquired knowledge and the gains of success to improve the society around him or her.

He/she knows (and is thankful) that Allah Subhana wa ta'ala has not forbidden earning a living, nor has He forbidden being wealthy. The astute Muslim understands and exercises Allah's order regarding the application of wealth, when He Subhana wa ta'ala has said, what translated means: "But seek, with that (wealth) which Allâh has bestowed on you, the home of the Hereafter, and forget not your portion of legal enjoyment in this world, and do good as Allâh has been good to you, and seek not mischief in the land. Verily, Allâh likes not the Mufsidûn (those who commit great crimes and sins, oppressors, tyrants, mischief-makers, corrupts)" (Al-Qasas 28:77).

The entrepreneurial Muslim has taken the steps, with full trust in Allah, to break free from the restraints of the typical 9 to 5. With salatul istikharah as his asset, he redefines and creates alternate means to pursue the wealth Allah has decreed and made lawful for him. He opens a multitude of avenues and possibilities to influence change in his personal life and in the lives of those around him. His Islamic ethos guides his intentions. He cultivates the individual strengths he has been blessed with and uses them to create positive impact on others. He emulates goodness because he reads the words of his Lord, which translated mean: " You are the best nation produced [as an example] for mankind. You enjoin what is right and forbid what is wrong and believe in Allah." (Ali 'Imran 3:110)

He finds strength in pursuing the freedom of the entrepreneur's life. The strength and ability to do more, be more and offer more. He carries the words that Abu Hurayrah has narrated that the Prophet (peace be upon him) said: "The strong believer is better and more beloved to Allah than the weak believer, while there is good in both. Guard over that which benefits you, seek Allah's Assistance, and don't lend yourself to things devoid of benefit, and if something befalls you, then don't say 'If I only would have done such and such,' rather say Allah decreed this and He does what He wills,' for verily the phrase 'If I would have' makes way for the work of the Devil" (Sahih Muslim).

The Muslim entrepreneur is optimistic because he knows that his ventures are in the Hands of his Lord. He has glimpsed the nuance, the immensity of Allah's favor, by realizing that the wealth and the opportunities he has been given are not to be wasted away in uncertainty or idleness but should instead be spent in an effort to attain the Hereafter, in an effort to please Allah.

May Allah make us of those who create benefit from the opportunities and the blessings He bestows on us. May He make us of those whose intentions are pure for His sake. May He make us of those whose legacy is one of beneficial contribution to the Ummah.

May He grant us the good of this life, the good of the hereafter, and may He protect us from the fire of Hell. Ameen.

Irada Abdul-Hadi

Lightning Source UK Ltd.
Milton Keynes UK
UKOW02f2225041016

284480UK00001B/3/P